D1501705

Medium

© Glamour Shots Shipleys Grant

About the Author

Konstanza Morning Star is an ordained Spiritualist minister, certified medium, and national Spiritualist teacher. She is also a shamanic practitioner. She holds a bachelor of arts degree from Newcomb College and a master of public health degree from Tulane University.

Konstanza brings comfort to the bereaved, facilitates healing on both sides of life, and guides clients through thorny life situations with evidential mediumship readings and séances in person, over the telephone, and via Skype. She works with an international clientele from all walks of life. She has taught mediumship and psychic development in the Greater Washington, DC, area since 2009. She is available to teach workshops throughout the United States. Her website is https://www.silverspringoflight.com/.

KONSTANZA MORNING STAR

Medium

a STEP-BY-STEP-GUIDE

to COMMUNICATING

with the SPIRIT WORLD

133.91 Star

Medium

Star, Konstanza Morning.
$15.99   30519009860589

Llewellyn Worldwide
Woodbury, Minnesota

PROPERTY OF
HIGH POINT PUBLIC LIBRARY
HIGH POINT, NORTH CAROLINA

Medium: A Step-by-Step Guide to Communicating with the Spirit World © 2016 by Konstanza Morning Star. All rights reserved. No part of this book may be used or reproduced in any manner whatsoever, including Internet usage, without written permission from Llewellyn Publications, except in the case of brief quotations embodied in critical articles and reviews.

FIRST EDITION
Second Printing, 2016

Book design by Bob Gaul
Cover images by iStockphoto.com/6166893/©DeepGreen
            iStockphoto.com/65876861/©soleg
            iStockphoto.com/61553438/©Ekaterina_P
Cover design by Ellen Lawson
Chapter images by iStockphoto.com/6166893/©DeepGreen
            iStockphoto.com/65876861/©soleg
Editing by Rhiannon Nelson

Llewellyn Publications is a registered trademark of Llewellyn Worldwide Ltd.

Library of Congress Cataloging-in-Publication Data
Names: Star, Konstanza Morning, 1962– author.
Title: Medium : a step-by-step guide to communicating with the spirit world / Konstanza Morning Star.
Description: First Edition. | Woodbury : Llewellyn Worldwide, Ltd, 2016. | Includes bibliographical references.
Identifiers: LCCN 2016012772 (print) | LCCN 2016013867 (ebook) | ISBN 9780738748139 | ISBN 9780738749327
Subjects: LCSH: Spiritualism. | Mediums.
Classification: LCC BF1261.2 .S73 2016 (print) | LCC BF1261.2 (ebook) | DDC 133.9/1—dc23
LC record available at http://lccn.loc.gov/2016012772

Llewellyn Worldwide Ltd. does not participate in, endorse, or have any authority or responsibility concerning private business transactions between our authors and the public.

All mail addressed to the author is forwarded, but the publisher cannot, unless specifically instructed by the author, give out an address or phone number.

Any Internet references contained in this work are current at publication time, but the publisher cannot guarantee that a specific location will continue to be maintained. Please refer to the publisher's website for links to authors' websites and other sources.

Llewellyn Publications
A Division of Llewellyn Worldwide Ltd.
2143 Wooddale Drive
Woodbury, MN 55125-2989
www.llewellyn.com

Printed in the United States of America

Contents

In loving memory of my father
and my beloved grandparents.

To all my students and clients and their spirit loved ones.

Acknowledgments

My heartfelt gratitude goes to:

- + My mother, for encouraging my love of reading and writing.

- + Aubrey Greer and Dylan Greer, for their love, encouragement, and enthusiasm. I love you.

- + George Greer, for seeing the writer in me and knowing I could write a book.

- + Kristin Donnan, for polishing the manuscript, fixing awkward constructions, spotting areas that needed elaboration or clarification, and guiding me through the process of preparing a manuscript.

- + The editors and staff at Llewellyn Worldwide, Ltd.

- My teachers and mentors: Reverends B. Anne Gehman, Leonard Justinian, Judith Rochester, Barbara "Bunny" Starr, Patricia Stranahan, and Stella Upton.

- Will McCarty, for suggesting that I write a book based on my workshops.

- Chesleigh Jonker, for input on various aspects of the manuscript.

- Dana and Shana Robinson for their insights on spirit possession.

- Nicolyn "Nikki" Green and Michael Hunter for reading earlier drafts of this manuscript.

- Deborah Harrigan, for good company, laughter, meals, and prayers.

- Marilyn and Knox Hayes and the members of the Drum Circle for their generous spiritual support.

- The ministers and members of the Center for Spiritual Enlightenment, NSAC.

- My father and grandparents, for working with me from the spirit side of life.

- My spirit guides, for always coming through for me and for providing insight at the right time.

- My students and clients; you are my teachers.

- The Great Mystery for this amazing life on our beautiful planet Earth.

Introduction

People often assume that you need to possess a special gift to be a medium. I believe that mediumship is a natural human skill, and that it can be developed just like you can learn how to read, write, calculate math, draw, drive a car, or play an instrument. None of us was born knowing any of these things, yet all of us managed to acquire most of these skills.

It is true: There are the Mozarts of this world who can compose music at the very tender age of five, and there are children who are naturally sensitive to spirit communication. Just as Mozart had to learn to play the piano and write music, the Mozarts of mediumship at some point must invest effort and discipline into unfolding their gifts.

Just because someone remembers being able to perceive the spirit world in childhood does not mean this person is going to be a better medium than those who discover their gifts at a later age. Someone who learned to play the guitar at age eight is not always going to be better or more gifted than someone who learned to play the instrument at age thirty-five or fifty-five.

In fact, I would say that the majority of mediums discover their gifts as adults. For example, one of my students is a neonatal intensive care nurse in a big hospital on the East Coast. One day, as she sat beside a premature infant in a coma, the baby's spirit told her that everything would be okay and to just tell everyone to hang in there. The infant assured the nurse that she would make it—and she did! Another example involves a friend who took Reiki training. On day two of coaching, he realized that a spirit healer was standing next to him and was giving him information about the fellow student he was practicing on. A third medium discovered her gift during her career as a funeral director. All of these individuals turned into fine mediums, though none of them remember any outstanding abilities or experiences during their childhoods.

How This Book Will Help You

This book will teach you how to connect with the spirit world in a straightforward, step-by-step process. Each step builds on the previous one, and you are introduced to key concepts as you go. You will learn how to develop your own innate gift of spirit communication, how mediumship works, how the spiritual senses work, how to establish a spiritual foundation to support your mediumship, and what constitutes compelling evidence of the survival of consciousness beyond the change called death.

A key element of this book that sets it apart from others of this genre is its quantity of specific and useful detail—detail that allows insight into what mediums experience in their minds and bodies as they engage in spirit contact. By describing how mediums perceive the spirit people through the spiritual senses, I will help you begin to understand what to look for in your own development. I draw on not only my own experience, but also on the experience of typical student mediums.

Most people don't think they have the ability to communicate with the spirit world, simply because they don't know what to look for. They expect to see their deceased loved ones just as they would perceive a person in the physical realm. Once they are aware of what to look for—and they commit to regular practice—students are able to connect with the spirit people.

How to Use This Book

I recommend you read the book from start to finish instead of jumping into random individual chapters. The material progressively builds upon fundamental concepts, and it's best to have the base knowledge before you skip around.

Take your time to become familiar with each of the steps involved in connecting with the spirit people. For easy reference, you might want to bookmark the pages with the individual steps as you go.

This book also includes a lot of techniques and exercises to help you sharpen your skills. Make these practices a part of your life, because they represent the spiritual foundation upon which mediumship is built. Repeat the exercises often.

Record each practice and exercise in a journal dedicated to the development of your mediumship. Throughout the months and years of its unfolding, record the impressions and communications you receive from the spirit world. On days when you feel that things just aren't happening fast enough, your journal will help you look back and realize how far you've come.

If possible, sign up for a development circle with a qualified teacher and commit to attending each session (chapter 13, "Development Circles and Home Circles").

Remember all the practice you had to put into perfecting your ability to walk, talk, read, and write, and the many hours of practice involved in learning how to play your favorite instrument or whatever other skill you've developed. So practice, practice, practice! And, most of all, have a lighthearted attitude and have fun with it.

The Rewards of Mediumship

The rewards of mediumship development are manifold. They include:

+ *Access to help from the spiritual realms.* As your mediumship develops, you will come to understand that you are always surrounded by loving helpers ready to assist you with any given task or challenge.

+ *Heightened sense of joy and appreciation for life.* Contact with the spirit world makes you realize that you are part of something larger and that your life experience is based on natural law, order, and purpose. It will help you live more fully and joyfully.

+ *Expanded perspective of life's challenges.* When you realize that you live in an orderly, purposeful universe, you will get in the habit of viewing life's challenges as opportunities to grow and expand beyond your current limits.

+ *Comfort to the bereaved.* When you develop your gift of mediumship, you will be able to comfort the bereaved. Also, your ability to connect with the spirit world will nurture and sustain you during times when your own loved ones die.

+ *Knowledge of the continuity of life removes the fear of death.* When you realize that physical death is merely a birth into an expanded state of being, you no longer fear death. You realize that life is eternal and that you are going to be reunited with loved ones who passed before you.

A Few Things to Keep in Mind

Throughout the book I use the words "God," "Great Mystery," "Great Spirit," and "Infinite Intelligence" to refer to the divine source of the universe. These terms are simply most comfortable to me. Please feel free, though, to substitute names that are most comfortable and familiar to you. For example, if you normally pray to the Divine Mother, or to the Goddess, or to Allah, or to the Source of All that Is, then use these forms of address instead of mine.

Also, as you start out on the honorable path of mediumship development, please realize that you are very much like an artist who is in the process of creating something beautiful. Under all circumstances, you must be gentle with yourself and refrain from negative self-criticism.

Please be patient. The path of the medium is full of thousands of baby steps that add up over time. And, as with everything else in life, it's the journey of discovery that counts, not the final destination. In mediumship, there is no final destination or bed of laurels to stretch out and rest on.

My Path As a Medium

I was able to perceive the spirit people at a young age. And because this was natural to me, it took some years before I realized that I was seeing things other kids did not. After a particularly bruising morning at elementary school where one of my classmates started howling, "Konstanza sees dead people!" and the rest of the class hooligans joined in a cacophonous chorus, I had enough. I just wanted to be "normal." And so the gift departed. I had sent it away, and Infinite Intelligence respected my free will.

It didn't return for thirty-some years, when in 2001—on a Tuesday morning at four—my deceased grandmother stood by the foot of my bed. I was living in Conakry, Guinea, at the time. The odd thing was that my grandmother looked like a schoolgirl about eleven years old, yet I recognized her instantly. Years later, I would learn that the spirit people often assume the appearance they had at the time in their life when they were happiest. Spirit people also often show themselves to a medium in the form that their loved one on earth, also known as the sitter, would best remember them. If the medium described them at unfamiliar ages or in unfamiliar settings, the sitter would probably have no clue who they are.

I do not recall specific events that precipitated the encounter with my deceased grandmother, except that I had begun to read books on spirituality and felt increasingly drawn toward mysticism.

In the years after the encounter with my grandmother, I experienced other occasions of spontaneous spirit contact. Finally, one day in 2004 I decided that it was time to attend a Spiritualist church and learn more. A year later, in early August 2005, a church member introduced me to a development circle held by one of the ministers at the church. I was floored when three spirit people presented themselves to me during my very first day in the circle, and the sitters in the circle validated every piece of information the spirits provided.

At the time, though, I was unable to hold a spirit link for more than a few seconds at most. I had no clue how to go about receiving additional information from the spirit visitors or how to resolve the various problems that can occur during a mediumship session. Still, I was off to what I considered a glorious start, and I kept at it. I attended that circle every Monday night for three years. During this time I also attended private home circles. I have now sat in circles for more than a decade, and I know that I will do so for the rest of my physical life.

I am an ordained Spiritualist minister, national Spiritualist teacher, and certified medium through the National Spiritualist Association of Churches (NSAC). I have been teaching mediumship and psychic development classes and circles since 2009. This book grew from my own mediumship development experiences, from the thousands of readings that I have given, from my years of teaching circles and workshops, and from inspiration from my spirit helpers. It is my sincere wish that this book helps you open the door to your own connection with the spiritual realms.

1

How Mediumship Works

Before we delve into the nuts and bolts of developing mediumship, let us define what a medium is. The *NSAC Spiritualist Manual* defines a medium as a person "whose organism is sensitive to the vibrations from the spirit world and through whose instrumentality, the people in the spirit world are able to convey messages and produce the phenomena of Spiritualism."[1]

I love this definition, because it makes it clear that for spirit communication to occur, three components must be in place: (1) a person in the spirit world with a desire to communicate; (2) a person in the physical realm who desires to hear from his or her deceased loved ones (I'll call this person the sitter or

---

1   The National Spiritualist Association of Churches, *NSAC Spiritualist Manual* (NSAC, 2004), 2.

the recipient); and (3) a person called a medium who is able to facilitate contact between earth and heaven. In other words, mediumship is always cooperation among medium, sitter, and spirit world. If one of these components is missing, there will be no spirit communication.

The ability to connect with the people in the spirit world distinguishes a medium from a psychic. All mediums are psychic, but not all psychics are mediums. Mediums connect with the spirit world through mental mediumship, a phenomenon where the medium holds a live conversation with the spirit people. Mediums receive pertinent and uniquely identifying information about the spirit communicator through the spiritual senses (chapter 5, "The Spiritual Senses"). They do not use tools such as Ouija boards, runes, crystal balls, or tarot cards to facilitate dialogue with the spirit people. Psychics, on the other hand, often use tools to access general information regarding the life of their sitter.

The purpose of mediumship is to bring evidence of the survival of consciousness beyond the change called death, and to thus bring healing and comfort to the bereaved. Mediums provide this evidence when they supply detailed insight and information about the spirit communicator that only the spirit person and his loved ones on earth would know (chapter 11, "Evidence and Spirit Messages"). And of course, once people realize that physical death is not the end of existence, they begin to live more consciously, and their awareness shifts from matters like the daily rat race and competition for material goods to what really matters in life.

Spirit Communication Is Said to Be Like Radio

Radio waves are invisible, electromagnetic waves that travel at the speed of light through space over great distances. Mediums, like radio receivers, pick up the unseen vibrations from the invisible spirit world that surrounds us. Just as you have to turn the dial of your radio for optimum reception of your favorite station, mediums have to shift their awareness from their ordinary consciousness and concentrate on receiving information from the spirit world.

Radio wave frequencies are categorized as short-, medium-, and long-range. Mediums, based on how developed their gift is, also have a certain range of spirit communicators with whom they are able to connect. Mediums can only communicate with spirit people who are "broadcasting" at an energy frequency that the medium can receive. That explains why no medium, no matter how gifted, can connect with all the spirit people.

Also, keep in mind that radio waves cannot penetrate very dense matter and thus can be blocked. The same is true for spirit communication. The spirit people are unable to broadcast through dense matter such as negativity, fear, doubt, and heavy emotions. Mediums can be blocked from connecting with the spirit world when they hold certain fears, attitudes, anger, or negativity.

As a beginning medium, you will have a much narrower range of reception than those who have been sitting in development circles for a number of years. You might count yourself lucky if you are able to give a couple pieces of information about your spirit contact. Often, though, you might find that you cannot perceive the spirit people with great precision. And after delivering a short message, your energy is probably spent, and you are done for that session. This is because it takes great concentration and focus to hold a connection with the spirit people.

Expanding Your Range

With time and experience, you will be able to communicate across a wide range of the spirit realm. Mediumship is very much like a muscle that gradually builds and gets stronger. Physical muscles are fueled by the food we eat. Your mediumship, on the other hand, is fueled and nourished through spiritual practices, including prayer, meditation, and correct application of the natural laws that govern spirit communication.

The Foundation of Mediumship Is Natural Law

It is important to realize that even though the spirit world is all around us, the spirit people, too, struggle in their attempts to communicate with a medium. The following passage, attributed to psychical researcher Frederic W.H. Myers, illustrates his difficulties as he attempted to convey information from the spirit world to three gifted mediums on different continents:

> "I am trying amid unspeakable difficulties. It is impossible for me to know how much of what I send reaches you. I feel as if I had presented my credentials—reiterating the proofs of my identity in a wearisomely repetitive manner. The nearest simile I can find to express the difficulty of

sending a message [from the spirit world] is that I appear to be standing behind a sheet of frosted glass, which blurs sight and deadens sound, dictating feebly to a reluctant and somewhat obtuse secretary. A feeling of terrible impotence burdens me."[2]

When you first apply for a learner's permit, the Department of Motor Vehicles makes sure that you know the traffic laws so that you and others will travel as safely as possible as you venture onto the roads of your neighborhood. Likewise, before venturing further into your ability to communicate with the spirit world, it is important that you understand the natural laws of mediumship. Application of these laws will help you create favorable conditions that keep you safe, nurture your gifts, and allow the spirit people to transmit pertinent information efficiently.

Following the description of most of the natural laws is a practice to help you apply it to your mediumship practice. As the word "practice" implies, I encourage you to incorporate these methods into your daily life so they become second nature. You might like some practices more than others, but I encourage you to work with them several times a week for at least three or four months. Record the results of each practice in your journal.

Occasionally, if you feel stuck in your development, or if for some reason your enjoyment of your gift has gone stale, review

---

2 Interpretive Introduction by Jeffrey Mishlove, PhD, *Human Personality and Its Survival of Bodily Death* by F.W.H. Myers (Hampton Roads Publishing Company, Inc., 2001), xii.

the laws of mediumship. Often you will find that you have forgotten to honor one of the natural laws. As soon as you start to apply them in your life, your mediumship will flow again.

The Law of Conservation of Energy

This law explains that the total energy of a system is constant, even though the system itself experiences internal changes. Water, for example, can assume liquid, frozen, and vapor states. With regard to mediumship, this law explains the continuity of life beyond physical death.

When a person dies, the physical body decomposes and its minerals return to the soil. The spiritual aspect that had inhabited the physical body and loved jazz, chocolate croissants, and T.S. Eliot returns to the spirit world. In other words, the spark of life that animated the physical body is neither lost nor destroyed—and it does not forget its personal identity or life experience.

This is important, because in life you are a spirit, just as are the people in the spirit world. The only difference between you and them is the fact that your spirit is currently cloaked in a physical body. But you are not your body. You are spirit. As spirit you can access the spirit realms, though chances are that no one has ever told you that.

The Law of Vibration

Communication between people on earth and the people in the spirit world functions through the Law of Vibration: everything in the universe exists in varying degrees of vibration or motion.

The physical realm, by its dense and solid nature, is characterized by a lower-energy frequency, called "vibration," than the spirit world. When the spirit people want to communicate through a medium, they have to lower their energy. The spirit people accomplish this by thinking about life on earth. As a medium, on the other hand, you have to raise your energy so that you can peek through the proverbial veil that separates the two worlds. You basically have to create a lighthearted, joyful, positive spiritual atmosphere inside yourself that helps you transcend the boundaries of the physical realm. It is easier to connect with the spirit world when your life is stable and when you feel good about yourself, because it places you in a naturally higher vibration.

Occasionally, I have met people who want to develop mediumship primarily because they are desperate to stay in touch with a close loved one who has recently died. Although their urgency is understandable, I sometimes have to tell them to wait awhile before attempting to learn mediumship. When you are recently bereaved and heartbroken, you are often sad, even depressed. Such emotions create what I describe as a kind of energetic fog that makes it virtually impossible for a person in this state to connect with the spirit world. A third-party medium, though, would have no problem connecting with your spirit loved ones on your behalf until you are in a more energetically balanced state.

Of course, there are exceptions to every rule. For some people, bereavement can act as a catalyst that opens up their ability to perceive the spirit people. This tends to be true for people who already have at least a rudimentary spiritual practice, even if that practice is decades old. Grief pulls us closer to God. During the most wretched moments of our lives, as we reach for God in prayer, we can experience a sense of upliftment and comfort that is beyond understanding. As we pray, we find that suddenly, magically, the veil between the two worlds has lifted and we are suddenly aware of the presence of our spirit loved ones.

Practice: Monitor Your Vibration through Self-Observation

For the next week, throughout each day, every hour, briefly stop what you are doing and check in with how you are feeling. For example, do you feel happy, joyful, lighthearted, anxious, frustrated, depressed, tense, peevish, or angry? Name the feeling and assign a number to it ranging from positive ten (+10) to negative ten (-10). Let zero simply be neutral. Give positive feelings a positive rating, and assign a negative value to unpleasant emotions. Record the feeling and the number you've assigned in your notebook. At the end of the week, review your notes. You will find that positive feelings correspond to a high vibration and negative feelings to a low vibration.

If you find that you have been spending significant amounts of time experiencing low-vibration feelings, don't despair. Continue to practice self-observation and continue to apply all the natural laws listed below. In addition, imagine switching the dial on your "inner radio" and selecting an "inner channel" that plays a positive program. Eventually you will be able live in a vibration that is conducive to easy spirit contact.

However, should you find yourself permanently depressed or stuck in a negative pattern, please seek medical care. Therapy and medication can go a long way toward helping you break out of a despondent pattern. And no, medication will not interfere with your ability to communicate with the spirit world.

The Law of Attraction

Beginning mediums always want to know whether it is safe to open up to the spirit world. What about "bad" spirit people who might want to attach to them, follow them home, and make things go bump in the night?

Due to the Law of Attraction, most people do not have to worry about attracting unpleasantness from the spirit world. The Law of Attraction states that like attracts like. Birds of a feather flock together. People who share similar qualities and interests are drawn to one another. This is true in the physical realm as well as in the spirit world.

The fact is that you will attract only spirit people and helpers that are like you in some way and with whom you have something in common: in the physical realm, for example, a lot of my friends are mediums with a deep commitment to spirituality. Years ago when my children were small, the majority of my friends were people who had small children.

The same is true for the spirit people. If you are a kind person with integrity who tries to live a healthy and conscientious life, devious, mischievous, or malicious spirit people of the lower astral realms (appendix A, "Earthbound Spirits and Conducting Spirit Rescue") won't find you attractive. Your spiritual energy would not be a match for them and they would not be interested in latching on to you.

Water seeks its own level. Like attracts like. So what would cause a person in the physical realm to draw in an earthbound negative influencing spirit? There has to be a commonality between the influencing spirit and the incarnated person. It usually is a habit that creates vulnerability and lowers the defenses of the incarnated person, such as alcoholism, drug abuse, S&M sex, vengefulness, etc. The influencing spirit is attracted to a person with such habits so that he or she can vicariously re-experience the thrills of physical life.

Your best protection against negative spirit influences is to be a person of integrity. Build your spiritual foundation and follow the guidelines presented in this book. Abstain from drug use, and don't hang out in places where people use and inebriate. Treat yourself with kindness and respect. Do not hurt or seek to control others. Refrain from manipulating and trying to bend others to your will. Conversely, don't blame others for everything that is wrong in your life. Take responsibility for yourself. Take charge of your life.

If you think that you might have picked up an errant spirit who is exerting an undue influence over you, I would suggest a round of self-clearing following Diana Burney's instructions from her book *Spiritual Clearings: Sacred Practices to Release Negative Energy and Harmonize Your Life*. You could also contact teachers from the Foundation for Shamanic Studies and schedule shamanic depossession.

The Law of Attraction also determines which types of spirit guides (chapter 7, "Spirit Guides and Helpers") you will attract. Spirit people elect to work with mediums who will present their messages in a manner that is in harmony with their own spiritual development. You will attract high-level spirit helpers when you do your best to live in accordance with high ethical standards and when you treat others as you would like to be treated.

However, if you are currently experiencing extremely negative life circumstances, or if you are going through severe antagonism and strife, it would be prudent to postpone commencement of your mediumship development until your life has become more balanced.

Until then, application of the natural laws combined with a regular prayer and meditation practice (chapters 3 and 4) will help you navigate your life challenges, lift your spirits, and prepare you for the time when you are ready to connect.

Practice: Review Your Connections

Take out your journal and pen. Think about a time when your circle of friends suddenly changed. What precipitated the change? Did you perhaps outgrow one another? Think about your current circle of friends. What drew you

together, and what continues to connect you? Examine
your relationships with significant people in your life and
see if you can detect patterns of the Law of Attraction.
Record your insights in your journal.

You have control over the Law of Vibration and the Law of Attraction not only through your interests and actions, but also through the choices that you make according to the Law of Free Will, as well as through your thoughts and attitudes as expressed through the Law of Thought.

The Law of Free Will

This law establishes that human beings have free will and that no spirit person is allowed to interfere with yours. No spirit person is able to possess or control you against your will. Over the past eleven years since I became disciplined about unfolding my mediumship, I have had contact with thousands of people who have sought me out for my spiritual services. During this time, only four cases of severe negative spirit interference came to my attention. All of them were caused by collusion, as the persons flat-out refused to send the possessing spirits away.

When I inquired into the reasons behind the refusals, one person said she had grown fond of the possessing spirit person and would feel lonely without her. Another sheepishly admitted that she would then have to take responsibility for her bad decisions and it was so much easier to blame her problems on an entity named "Ralph." A third person admitted that she enjoyed the drama and how she got to be the center of attention when she had one of her episodes with the controlling spirit. A fourth person confessed that her collaboration with an extremely nasty spirit kept her on disability payments so she didn't have to go to work. In other words, all four of them derived benefits from keeping the negative spirit around.

It is entirely up to you to choose the spirit company that you keep. If you don't like the company of a particular spirit person, then exercise your free will and firmly order this individual to go away.

The Law of Thought

You are probably not aware of it, but the people in the spirit world communicate through thought. If they want to go somewhere, they just think about where they want to be, and there they are. Because spirit communication is through thought, you must accept that your own thoughts are also fully visible, open, and accessible to the spirit people. There is no such thing as a private thought as far as they are concerned. Positive and encouraging thoughts lift your spirits and your vibration. Negative thoughts lower your vibration. Sadly, a lot of us are in the habit of engaging in depressing and negative self-talk. This kind of talk can very much get in the way of connecting with the spirit people.

The following practice is wonderful for helping us improve our self-talk and thoughts. Please note that you only have to be willing to release fear-based thoughts, harmful attitudes, and painful memories, and you can purge them from yourself. Repeat as often as you like.

Practice: Release Fear-Based Thoughts, Attitudes, Memories, and Experiences

Sit down, find a comfortable position, and close your eyes. Relax your body and your mind. Once you are in a state of relaxation, call upon your spirit helpers, the angels, and the Divine to assist you. Bring to mind a fear-based attitude that you are now willing to release—perhaps fear of not having enough, or fear of not being good enough. Ask yourself if there are some hurtful events or memories from the past that you are now *willing* to release. Once you have identified what you are *willing* to release, visualize or imagine that you are putting all these things into a box. Put a lid on the box and hand it over to your spirit helpers, angels, and God. Then, in the future, if you find your mind going back to these fears or memories, stop yourself and say: "I continue to release this situation. I will no longer dwell on it."

The Law of Thought states that thought is a powerful creative force. If a given thought is held long enough, it will eventually manifest in the physical realm. You should always tell yourself that you can learn and master anything that you put your mind to. You should always hold positive expectations and think well of yourself and your spiritual gifts.

Practice: Make Positive Affirmations

Take out your journal and create a list of positive affirmations that you are a medium, even though right now you might not yet be sure of it. Keep your statements simple, positive, and in the present tense. For example:

+ "I am open to contact with the spirit world."
+ "I am a medium."
+ "I help others with my spiritual gifts."
+ "I am a clear conduit for spirit communication."
+ "I clearly see, hear, sense, and feel the presence of the spirit people."
+ "I bring messages of comfort and healing to the bereaved."
+ "I am a clear channel for the love of spirit."

Read your list of statements aloud five times a day, and do so for several months. Any time doubt sets in, go back and read your affirmations aloud.

Get in the habit of thinking well of other people and develop the habit of giving others the benefit of the doubt. The people in the spirit world are drawn to mediums that are compassionate and nonjudgmental. You will be more attractive to the spirit people when they feel safe to express honestly who they were in life: human beings with human shortcomings.

Practice: Observe Yourself

During the next several weeks, practice some self-observation. Notice how you feel inside when you think kindly of someone. Conversely, notice how you feel when you are thinking negative or judgmental thoughts. What thoughts make you feel lighthearted and good about yourself? Can you find a way to replace the negative thought or attitude with a positive one or with one that gives the other person the benefit of the doubt? Record your observations in your journal.

While your mediumship skills are unfolding, the Law of Thought also stresses the importance of always seeing the proverbial glass as half-full! In our modern world of high-speed Internet, text messaging, and instant gratification, a lot of beginning mediums are impatient to get results. Sadly, that often means they aren't happy with the amount of spirit information that they receive. They might receive two or three very valid pieces of evidence, but then express deep disappointment that they are "only" receiving "so little." Instead, get in the habit of acknowledging and celebrating the smallest impressions you receive from the spirit world. If you approach mediumship with an attitude of "Wow, I am receiving so much good information," then your enthusiasm and happiness will open the gateway toward receiving more.

The Law of Service

This law states that our purpose on earth is to assist and serve humanity. Your purpose as a medium is to bring healing by providing evidence of the survival of consciousness beyond physical death. As long as your motivation for mediumship is to be an instrument for Spirit and to help others, you can be sure that your gift will unfold and that your spirit helpers will support your effort.

If your main motivation for developing mediumship is the lure of fame and fortune, think again. I can assure you that there are many better ways to get rich than being a medium.

It takes years to fully develop your gift and even then, mediumship can be fragile, as it depends on the cooperation among the medium, sitters, and the spirit people. Upsets in your health or personal life and difficult sitters can affect the quality of your work and your ability to support yourself as a medium. Besides, motivation for financial gain will not nourish your spirit during times when your ability takes a nosedive (chapter 15, "The Natural Cycles of Mediumship Development).

If you are motivated by a desire to be a light in the world and to help others, the Great Mystery will put you to good use. And if you are very lucky, fame and fortune might become accidental byproducts of your service to others.

Practice: Discover Motivation

Take out your journal and explore in writing your motivation for wanting to become a medium. What is stirring this heart's desire in you? In what ways can you begin to be of service to Spirit while you are developing your gift of mediumship?

When my mediumship falls into a rut, it is often because I have fallen behind in service to humanity. As an ordained Spiritualist minister, one of my duties includes preparing and giving the homily in our morning service. This is to be done on a regular basis, but without a strict schedule. Sometimes life gets in the way, and I don't get around to serving as speaker. I find that when I cut back on serving as speaker, my mediumship suffers. As soon as I sign up to speak, my mediumship again flourishes.

The Law of Service is about our willingness to be God's instruments, but without stipulating the terms of our service. We must seek to serve others not only through our mediumship, but also through performing other kinds of services that add value to others. Doing something positive for the sole purpose of doing it, instead of focusing on what's in it for you, will change your life in many positive ways.

Practice: Incorporate Service into Your Daily Life

What small actions—unrelated to mediumship—could you take in your daily life that would make life better for others? Get out your journal and write a list of numbers from one to twenty. Quickly fill in your ideas, without thinking too long and hard about each one. Work from your gut. For example:

- Take the trash to the curb for my neighbor.
- Let someone go ahead of me in the grocery line.
- Bring snacks to the office.
- Babysit my nephew.
- Pay the fee for the person behind me at the tollgate.

Commit yourself to doing something positive with a caring heart for at least one person every day.

The Law of Love

This law affirms that love is the key that opens the door to spirit communication. Love makes it possible for a spirit person who had a difficult relationship with the sitter to find the courage to come into the reading to make amends. Love can break the ice of resentment. While sitters might initially feel ambiguous about hearing from spirits who hurt them in life, they invariably experience profound healing when the spirit people are given the opportunity to have their say. As a medium, the spirit people are always drawn to you when you send them love and when you approach your sitters with a loving heart.

Practice: Locate Unconditional Love

Turn off the television and silence the telephone. Go into your sacred space, light a candle, and begin to relax.

Remember a time in your life when you experienced unconditional love. It could be the love you felt for your newborn baby, for a beloved parent, grandparent, or pet. With each breath, fill yourself with unconditional love. Let it fill your heart. Extend the feeling of unconditional love beyond your physical body into the room around you, and to all the people in your life. You can take this exercise a step further and extend your unconditional love to Mother Earth and all of life. Spend as much time as you like inhaling and exhaling unconditional love. Afterward, record your experience in your journal.

Repeat this exercise as often as you wish.

The Law of Cause and Effect

This law reminds us that every action, good or bad, produces a reaction. We reap what we sow. You will get out of your mediumship what you put into it. Just like you won't learn how to draw unless you draw regularly, you won't develop mediumship if you don't invest the required time and effort.

Practice: Track Efforts and Results

Think back to a time when you achieved a goal that you worked hard for. How much effort did it take? How long did it take to accomplish your goal? How did your attitude help you achieve your goal? What helped you persevere through times of difficulty? Can you see the connection between cause and effect? Record your reflections in your journal.

Also, because mediums are naturally sensitive, you must be mindful of the energies that you send out into the world, because what you send out will come back to you. Mediums are easily affected and shut down by discord and disharmonious conditions in their lives. My experience shows that the best policy—though not always the easiest—is to live by the Golden Rule: "Do unto others as you would have them do unto you." It avoids a lot of unnecessary conflict and helps you live a good life. When friction with others remains at a minimum, our ability to open to the spirit world flourishes.

The Law of Control

This law affirms that mediums are always in control of their mediumship. As mediums, we purposefully connect with the spirit world. When we are finished with a reading or a public demonstration, we purposefully close the connection. This way, we can enjoy our life in the physical realm without constant intrusions from the other side. When I go out to dinner with friends, walking in Rock Creek Park, or to the grocery store, I don't want to be bothered by anybody's spirit people. Because I exercise control over my mediumship, my spirit helpers know that unless I'm giving a reading or am about to teach or give a public demonstration, I am not to be contacted by the spirit people.

One thing mediums don't have control over is whether a particular spirit person is going to come through for a sitter. This is because the spirit people have free will, just as you do. If your Aunt Marge invites you to a party, you can either accept or decline the invitation. The same can be true for the spirit people.

However, you do have control over whether or not you wish to engage in contact with a spirit person. You can always terminate a spirit contact, if you wish.

Practice: Find the On/Off Switch

Whenever you wish to connect with the spirit world, imagine that there is a little invisible switch at your temple. When you flip the switch to the "on" setting, it's time to receive spirit contact. When you flip the switch to the "off" position, the connection to the spirit world is terminated until you turn it on again.

The Law of Correspondence

This law aligns with the Law of Thought. It states that our outer world is a reflection of our inner world, and vice versa. Another way of putting it is, "As above, so below."

Please know that as you take steps toward spiritual growth and your mediumship unfolds, the Great Mystery and your spirit helpers will meet you more than halfway. It is my experience that whatever it is that we would like to do in life, Infinite Intelligence supports us and helps create conditions that assist us in our endeavor. When you are aligned with the Law of Correspondence, doors open and opportunities present themselves.

You will set the Law of Correspondence into action when you hold a strong desire to be a medium and when you pull closer to the Great Mystery through praying and meditating. The next three chapters will help you implement a regular prayer and meditation practice.

Common Beginner's Concerns and Setbacks

Application of the natural laws combined with the other practices discussed in this book will go a long way toward opening your natural ability to communicate with spirits. However, beginners often harbor attitudes and fears that tend to get in the way. Here are the most common concerns:

Fear of Coming Out of the Psychic Closet

Beginning mediums often worry that family and friends will think they are crazy when they hear they are learning mediumship. Some fear their fiancées or spouses would dump them if they knew.

It is true our significant others, friends, and family members might not understand why we suddenly want to talk to dead people. My ex-husband used to wonder, "Aren't there enough people in the physical world that you can talk to?"

Beginning mediums often discover their relationships begin to change as a result of opening up to the spiritual realms. It is up to you to decide how much you want to share about the unfolding of your gifts with your family and friends. There is a verse in the Bible that warns, "Do not give that which is holy to the dogs, nor cast your pearls before the swine, lest they trample them under their feet, and turn around and tear you in pieces."

So don't proselytize about life after death. And never try to prove yourself to a skeptical friend or loved one. Instead, apply your spiritual knowledge to improve your own life and to help others. Become a better friend and a more compassionate partner. In time, your friends will notice you have changed. Remember, even when people are curious, you don't owe them an explanation.

Fear of Lack of Ability and Fear of Failure

Another very common beginner's worry is that out of all the people in the world, you are the only one who totally lacks any sort of psychic and mediumistic ability. Sometimes the fear of failure is so deep-seated that the fear itself becomes a fortress that keeps the spirit vibes from piercing through.

Creativity teacher Julia Cameron, author of *The Artist's Way: A Spiritual Path to Higher Creativity*, reminds us that in order to succeed, we first must be willing to fail. The same is true for mediumship.

If you want to be a medium, you have to be willing to experience times where nothing happens or where you get things wrong. So don't let fear of failure stop you. Instead, give yourself full permission to be the least talented medium in the world, and plunge ahead anyway. It might take months, but unless you give it a try, you will never know the gifts that lie dormant within you.

Great Ambition and Unrealistically High Expectations

Closely related to the fear of failure is enormous ambition and impossibly high expectations. Don't get me wrong: I am not saying that you shouldn't desire to become the best medium you could possibly be. But you must be careful not to set the stakes too high.

Occasionally, I have a student who expects to perform at a stellar level every time from the first try onward. When such ambitious beginning mediums get something wrong or when they are not progressing as fast as they think they should, they berate themselves and get very frustrated. This, of course, takes the joy out of mediumship and makes it miserable.

If you were just starting to learn how to play the piano, you wouldn't expect yourself to flawlessly play an entire Beethoven concerto after your first piano lesson. And you certainly wouldn't expect to practice without hitting bum notes. Mediumship is no different. Check your expectations, keep an open mind and a positive attitude, and know that with time you will progress.

Trying Too Hard

Some students tell me when they first started to take my classes they often tried too hard and the very act of trying so hard created a block for them. When they decided to stop trying and just let things happen, suddenly the block disappeared and they connected with the spirit people.

This is true for all mediums, beginners and professionals alike, myself included. Sometimes when I lead a development circle at the end of a long, tiring day I think: "Tonight I will only facilitate and coach my students, but I'm not going to bring through anyone's spirit people. I just don't have the energy for it." Sure enough, that's usually the night when, against all of my expectations and without even trying, I experience wonderful spirit contact full of phenomenal evidential information.

When we let ourselves off the hook, we create the relaxed atmosphere within us that allows mediumship to flourish. When we give ourselves space and get out of own way, spirit contact occurs spontaneously.

Attitude Matters

It is best to cultivate a positive attitude toward yourself and your ability to connect with the spiritual realms. Always keep an open mind and an open heart. Develop a lighthearted and fun-loving attitude toward mediumship development.

It is important to remember that spirit communication is not so much about doing something or forcing things to happen. It is about being calm, relaxed, passive, and open so we can notice the presence of the spirits.

2
Creating Sacred Space

It is helpful to create a sacred space for your interaction with the spirit world, including meditation and the processes and exercises in this book. The spiritual energies gradually accumulate, and they will support you as your gifts develop. Some of you might have the luxury of setting an entire room aside for your spiritual work. Others might count themselves lucky if they can carve out a small but inviting corner of a shared bedroom. When I first started meditating, my children were young and we lived in a small house. Every morning after my husband went to work and my children left for school, I would clear off the dining room table, light a candle and some incense, and meditate in my usual seat at the table. That was my sacred space, and only I knew about it.

To make your space sacred and inviting, at a minimum you will need:

- *A clean uncluttered space.* It doesn't mean that you need to go on a major housecleaning mission each time you want to meditate or try a process from this book. But a clean and organized space makes it more tempting to sit and meditate. Cluttered or dirty areas do not promote inner peace or clarity, and might distract you.

- *Regardless of the season, open the windows prior to commencing your spiritual work and let in fresh air.* This removes old, stuck energy and sends the universe the message you are ready to experience something new. Also, the extra oxygen in fresh air will make it easier for you to stay awake.

- *Keep living plants or cut flowers in your sacred space.* They'll lift the energy of the room and brighten your mood, making it easier to connect with the spiritual realm.

You might also wish to:

- *Set up an altar.* Keep it simple. Place on it only things that have deep personal meaning to you and that draw you closer to the Divine. Objects could include a feather that you found on a walk, a stone from the campsite where you've spent a magical night under the stars, a pinecone from your last hike, shells from the beach, a peony from your garden, or a small handful of soil from your favorite place on earth. You don't need to buy tchotchkes, crystals, statues, Tibetan bells, fancy candles, and so forth. More isn't necessarily better. Interact with the items on your altar by handling and cleaning them. Periodically switch them out. This keeps your altar alive and symbolizes your active, living connection with the Great Mystery.

+ *Light a candle.* This sets the mood and gives you the cue that it is time to step out of your ordinary consciousness.

+ *Burn incense or sage.* This sacred herb of the Native Americans is known for its clearing and protective properties. Catholics have been burning frankincense in their services for millennia, and Hindus burn incense for their morning prayers. Experiment with different brands and scents to find one that appeals to you. (If you have allergies or sensitivity to such materials, do not use them, for your discomfort will interfere with your meditation.)

+ *Experiment with light.* Some people find that different levels of light facilitate an easier connection with the spiritual realms. Some people like to meditate in the sunlight, others in a slightly darkened room. Try meditating in bright and dark rooms to determine what works for you.

+ *Soft, relaxing music.* This can help you unwind and drown out external auditory distractions. However, some people regard music as a distraction, and they prefer to connect with Spirit in complete silence. When you meditate to music, just make sure that it is not too energetic. You might want to go to iTunes or Amazon.com and listen to samples of music by a German musician named Deuter. His music is spiritually uplifting and soothing, and supports altered states of consciousness.

3

The Role of Prayer
in Mediumship

Your mediumship will blossom with a regular prayer practice because it will bring you into alignment with the Great Spirit and the web of life. The Great Mystery, Infinite Intelligence is the Great Spirit that permeates everything that exists, including people, animals, plants, trees, rocks, rivers, oceans, mountains, the sky, planets, and stars. When we get into the habit of praying, we align ourselves with that overarching permeating spirit. It begins to flow through us in a broader capacity, expanding our own spirit and capacity to love and be compassionate toward others and ourselves. As these spiritual qualities expand within us, they open the doors for contact with the spirit world.

I have known several people whose ability to perceive the spirit people opened up when they began a prayer practice. None of these individuals spends inordinate amounts of time on prayer, yet each feels gently inspired to pray for others during the course of their day.

For example, one woman's walk to work leads her through her neighborhood cemetery. One morning she noticed the fresh grave of a male child and felt moved to pray for him and his grieving family. A few days later, on her way home, she experienced spontaneous communication from the deceased boy: He thanked her for her prayers and assured her they had helped.

Moving forward, she made a point to pray for those whose graves somehow drew her attention. As a result, she started to experience more spirit contact. Over time, her mediumship has beautifully expanded. One day she noticed her previously harsh and hectic work environment had become more peaceful. She attributes the positive changes at work to her prayers on the way to work.

Another woman, an avid hiker, got into the habit of ending each hike with prayers for the health of Mother Earth and the animals that live upon her. Within a year, she became aware of animal spirits. This led her to become an animal communicator. Over time, her gift expanded to communication with deceased humans. She, too, has become a very talented medium.

How to Pray

For some people, the idea of prayer brings back memories of the doldrums of rote prayers forced upon them in Sunday school or parochial schools. Unless you feel an affinity for certain traditional prayers, you do not need to use them. Prayer works best when you use your own words. You do not need to use fancy or flowery language and you do not need to make lengthy prayers. Longer isn't necessarily better. What matters is that you pray with sincerity. What matters is that you feel in your heart the sincere desire for what you pray for.

Jump-Start Your Prayer Practice

People often say that prayer is talking to God, but I find that prayer doesn't always need to be a mental monologue. Any activity that inspires a deep reverie can be your prayer. It can occur spontaneously—as you drive across Chain Bridge in Washington, DC, and you spot a bald eagle diving into the Potomac River below, or when a particularly beautiful piece of music cracks you wide open. Vigorous cardiovascular exercise can also inspire reverie, when with each breath you feel a profound awe of the miracle of being alive.

You can purposefully engage in activities that touch your spirit and connect you with God. Below are a few exercises to help get you started. Feel free to engage in any and all of them, or similar ones of your own, whenever you wish.

Practice: Practice Gratitude

Perhaps you are unaccustomed to prayer and you don't know how to begin to pray. I suggest you start with gratitude for all the blessings in your life. Even if you are currently going through a rough patch, there is always something to be grateful for, whether it is that you are employed, or are blessed with a loving family, a dear friend, or good health. Perhaps you can simply appreciate the beauty of nature all around you. Gratitude opens the heart. It creates a great sense of joy, appreciation, and love, just as it reduces the illusion of separation from the Great Spirit.

Practice: Ask the Great Spirit to Awaken Your Heart in Love

Have you ever noticed what happens when you are in love? When your heart is opened in love for that special person, you cannot help but see beauty everywhere and in everyone. That is because love is the glue that connects us to everything around us. When we love, we feel the presence of God.

After you've made your request, it is important to back up your prayer with action. As you go about your day, make a conscious effort to be a caring, cheerful, loving presence to everyone you encounter. It won't be long before you realize something magical is happening in your life.

Practice: Go into Nature for Sunset Prayers

On a day when you are unhurried, and preferably alone, find a beautiful natural setting. Ensure you have whatever you need to be comfortable and focused. For example, even if it's a warm day, bring something warm to put on in case the temperature drops—you don't want the weather to distract you. Watch the entire sunset, from the time the sun sinks low in the sky until complete darkness falls. As the sun sets, give thanks for the abundance in your life. Thank the Great Mystery for the beauty of this earth. Pray for good health, healing, and well-being for all life on this planet. Let your prayer well up from deep inside you, in whatever way you desire. Ask the rays of the sun to take your prayer—and God's blessings—around the planet.

Practice: Make Evening Prayers in the Deep Woods

Find a quiet place in nature where you won't be disturbed by passersby, and make your prayers. Keep your eyes open as you pray. Give thanks for and pray for everything your eyes see. Continue praying with your eyes open wide, observing how nature responds. When you are finished praying, sit quietly and listen to the sounds of the woods surrounding you. When you feel the energy shift, record your experiences in your journal.

Practice: Take a Sacred Walk

Go for a walk in nature or in your local park, and ask God to walk with you. Ask God to let you experience the woods through the Great Mystery's eyes. With each step, know (or simply assume) that God is walking with you. With each breath, send your love and your thoughts to God. Give thanks for every step you take. Give thanks for your body and your health (even if it is not as perfect as you'd like it to be). Give thanks for the beauty all around as well as for the smells of nature. Walk slowly. Don't rush. Let each step be a prayer. Notice how this makes your walk different from an ordinary walk. Focus your mind on the presence of the Great Spirit. At the end of your walk, record your experience in your journal.

Practice: Pray for Everyone

Pray for everyone in a given situation. Pray that everyone's needs are taken care of. Pray that God will surround them with love. Pray they are given all the help they need at this time to move forward with their life missions. Pray that everything in their lives will be healed. Ask that God will look upon them with loving eyes and with compassion.

Make sure you include everyone you know in this prayer, especially the people whom you might not care for or with whom you experience difficulty. Include your greatest enemies. When you pray for everyone, including enemies, you will find that situations transform faster and more positively, because everyone receives what they need. Don't pray that people will change to your liking. Pray for their highest good and for their well-being.

Be sure to make notes in your journal about your progress in life as well as your relationship with them. Oftentimes when we start praying for others without trying to bend them to our advantage, our relationship with them begins to change positively. Praying for everyone is a wonderful way of expressing unconditional love, being a light to others, and transforming hardened attitudes.

Practice: Pray Everywhere

Daily life gives us many opportunities to engage in spontaneous prayer. Pray while you are stuck at a red light or when the rush-hour traffic crawls to a halt. Pray while you wait in the grocery store checkout line, or while you're at the gas station waiting for your tank to fill up. Take these short moments to "check in" with the Great Mystery—offer a short prayer of gratitude, or pray for those who are also in line with you, or just send loving thoughts to everyone in your environment.

Practice: Write Your Prayers

There can be situations in our lives that we obsess about. Perhaps you are worried about your brother's cancer, how to afford the new car that you so desperately need, or whether you'll ever have children. Get out your journal and a pen. Set ten minutes on a timer. Start writing your prayers. Don't worry about grammar or punctuation. Just write as fast as you can without stopping. Don't hold back, and pour your heart out! Don't stop writing until the timer rings. After you have written your prayer, release it from your heart and mind, knowing that help and guidance are on the way.

Practice: Decree Blessings

I hit upon this exercise after I moved into my apartment in 2012. One day as I prepared for my morning meditation, the neighborhood became particularly active. School buses stopped in front of my building and honked incessantly. The garbage truck pulled up and took forever to get aligned just so with the curb. The little terrier downstairs got agitated and started its incessant barking. I could feel my neck muscles tense in frustration—and then I suddenly decided to bless all the noisemakers. I sent a mental smile and hug as I thought, "Great Mystery, please bless the driver of the garbage truck. Bless the little dog downstairs. Bless the school bus and all who ride on it." With each blessing, I felt better, more relaxed, and joyful. Then something amazing happened: my neighbors all started to leave for work at once. As each door opened, I blessed the occupants. A brawl broke out downstairs. I blessed those involved. A toddler started to scream. I blessed her. Ambulances and fire trucks hurled down the street. One stopped below my balcony. I blessed them all. I continued blessing everyone and everything I heard. I realized the act of blessing brought on more people and situations that desperately needed to be blessed. Finally, once all the noise settled down, the Great Mystery blessed me with one of the most profound meditations I had ever had.

Prayer Confers Spiritual Protection

As a Spiritualist medium, I preface all my work with the spirit world with prayer. This ensures that only the highest and the best spirit communicators are going to connect with me and that the spirit messages serve the recipient's highest purpose.

There are different schools of thought as to whether it is necessary to specifically ask for protection during the opening prayer. Some mediums ask for protection and feel vulnerable if they don't. Others argue that if you ask for protection, you basically declare that there is something to fear. If you focus on what you fear, so the argument goes, you will attract it. Personally, I feel that when you invoke the Divine Presence in prayer, you are automatically protected and all is well.

I like to use the following invocation, also referred to as an opening prayer, whenever I wish to connect with the spirit world:

"Infinite Spirit, Great Mystery; please surround us with your love and light. Uplift our hearts and minds so that we may be cognizant of your loving presence. We miss our spirit loved ones, and we would like to visit with them today. Please make this visit possible. We ask that they will bring abundance of proof of the continuity of life as well as messages of comfort, guidance, encouragement, inspiration, or whatever might be needed at this time. Bring us into attunement with you, with one another, and with the spirit world. Thank you! Amen."

Feel free to use my prayer, if you like, or let it inspire your own invocation.

Questions & Answers

I tried prayer for a couple of days but I just can't get into it.

You are struggling because prayer is new to you. In the beginning, many people have a hard time warming up to it. Teresa of Ávila compared prayer to the cultivation of a garden: In the beginning, the soil is dry and full of weeds. It's as though you have to draw buckets of water from a well by hand. You can't sit still. You get distracted. You feel bored.

Once you make it past this difficult beginning stage, you begin to discover the rewards of prayer. Teresa compares this phase to the discovery of a wheel above the well: As you turn the crank, the buckets of water come up with much less effort. Your prayers flow and you begin to feel emotional and spiritual upliftment as you pray.

Over time, as you continue your prayer practice, the garden of your soul is watered by a spring or stream. Your desire for material things and pleasures dwindles. You experience an intense longing for union with the Great Mystery.

Finally, Teresa assures us, the garden of your soul is watered by rain. Your prayers are effortless. They pour out of you as you greet each moment with prayer. You experience profound spiritual insights and understanding that change your life in a new and positive direction. Manifesting your dreams is effortless, as you know that you are always supported in your endeavors.

I have found this to be true. The rewards of prayer are definitely worth the initial struggle, so I would suggest that you stop the inner argument and just stick with it.

How can one person's prayer really make a difference?
Once, in a meditation, my spirit guides showed me the power of prayer. Even though you might be praying alone in the privacy of your home, unsure if anyone or anything even listens, each prayer is powerful and makes a positive difference in the world. You might not realize it, but every prayer reverberates through the universe, affecting the entire web of life. This is similar to the ripples of a rock thrown into a body of water. The ripples expand and create motion across the entire water.

I grew up in a particular spiritual tradition. I feel most comfortable praying the formal prayers of that faith. Do I need to change how I pray in order to develop my mediumship?
Feel free to continue to pray your favorite prayers. You do not need to abandon your spiritual tradition in order to become a medium. However, I would suggest that you use or adapt the opening and closing prayers suggested in this book when you wish to engage with the spirit people.

You say I should pray. Do you mean that I should constantly ask God for favors?
No. Your prayers don't need to be a constant begging of favors from the Divine. You can hold a prayerful state of mind throughout the

day by noticing and appreciating the beauty of nature. A heart filled with gratitude also brings us into deep states of communion with the sacred realms. Both will help increase your sensitivity to and perception of the spiritual realms.

I was taught that I should only pray
for others and not for myself. Is that true?
No. There is nothing wrong with praying for others and praying for yourself. You are a sentient being who is just as deserving of divine assistance as the next person. We have free will, and no one has the right to interfere with our free will. This means that we need to ask for help when we want it. Never hesitate to pray for support in all of your endeavors.

What is the best and most effective way to pray?
The best prayers come from the heart. Pray like you mean it, and pour out your heart. Pray with passion and with love. Guru Paramahansa Yogananda said:

> Prayer in which your very soul is burning with desire for
> God is the only effectual prayer. You have prayed like that at
> some time, no doubt, perhaps when you wanted something
> very badly or urgently needed money—then you burned
> up the ether with your desire. That is how you must feel for
> God…and you will see that He will respond.[3]

---

3   Paramahansa Yogananda, *Man's Eternal Quest: Collected Talks & Essays on Realizing God in Daily Life* (Self-Realization Fellowship, 1982), 353.

4

Meditation and Attunement with the Divine

Meditation opens the door to the spirit world and to spiritual experiences. It is the fuel for mediumship. Indeed, without meditation you will not develop your mediumship. Spiritualist mediums, including those who were mediums from a tender age, meditate at least once a day. In addition to my morning meditation, I also prepare myself for each client reading with a twenty-minute meditation. For mediums, meditation is as essential to our spiritual well-being as food and water is to our physical body.

Meditation increases your awareness of and sensitivity to the subtle, gentle presence of the spirit people. Daily meditation leads to greater self-understanding. When you have insight into how your mind operates, you will become better at distinguishing true spirit communication from your imagination (chapter 8, "Is It Spirit Communication or Imagination?"). Meditation also teaches you to keep your mind focused. This is an essential skill for a good medium; spirit communication is often fleeting, and you will miss most of it if you cannot hold your focus.

The purpose and promise of meditation, however, is much grander than and goes far beyond spirit communication. Its aim is nothing less than your attunement with the Great Mystery, a process that allows Infinite Intelligence to express itself through you and touch the hearts and minds of all you come into contact with. As a medium, you want to be a hollow reed for the expression of a higher power.

Catholic nuns and monks have long known that meditation ultimately leads to communion and union with the Divine. For hundreds of years they have practiced a form of meditation called contemplative prayer. Contemplation is only taught in cloisters and monasteries. For instance, Teresa of Ávila, a Spanish saint who lived during the sixteenth century, was gifted time and time again with union with Christ during contemplation.

Lifelong practice of meditation provides you with greater levels of spiritual awareness, understanding, and compassion for yourself and others. Meditation brings us into contact with the Divine and leads to experiences of love that are beyond anything that can be experienced among humans on Earth.

Whenever you sit down to meditate, always seek out and merge with the divine presence. It does not matter whether you call the Divine presence God, Allah, Infinite Intelligence, Great Mystery, Source, All that Is, or Great Spirit. Your connection with the spirit world flows from this attunement with the Divine.

How to Prepare Yourself for Meditation and Mediumship

At its core, meditation is as simple as sitting down, closing your eyes, relaxing the body, and breathing in and out. Yet a little bit of preparation goes a long way in creating optimal conditions for meditation and mediumship.

- *Avoid alcohol and recreational drugs before meditation.* They chemically alter your perceptions and interfere with spirit communication. They may also attract earthbound spirits who are vicariously trying to re-experience earth-plane thrills.

- *Avoid heavy meals.* A full stomach kills meditation and mediumship. No spiritual phenomena will happen when your stomach is busy digesting a heavy meal. You want to have something light in your stomach—just enough so you won't get distracted with hunger, but not so much that you are even slightly full or uncomfortable.

- *If possible, spend some time in nature.* A walk in the park or sitting in the backyard, on the front porch, or on the balcony can put us in a frame of mind where we are more open to Spirit.

+ *Wear loose and comfortable clothing* so you can breathe freely. You might want to keep a shawl at hand in case you get cold during meditation.

+ *Banish all distractions* such as housemates, children, and disruptive pets. Turn off the television and the telephone. Put a "Do Not Disturb" sign on your door, and tell everyone not to interrupt you unless it is of dire importance.

+ *Write your to-do list or your shopping list before meditation* so you won't have to try to keep these things in mind while you meditate.

+ *Meditate roughly at the same time and in the same place each time.* The spiritual energies build up in that place over time. Before long, you will find that your spirit helpers are already waiting for you as you sit down for meditation.

How Much Time Should You Invest in Meditation?

It depends. When you first begin to meditate and practice the steps listed below, you are going to need more time, simply because the processes will be unfamiliar to you.

Also, each meditation is different. Some mornings you might meditate for fifteen minutes, other mornings for thirty minutes. Occasionally you might come out of meditation to find that an hour has flown by.

Give it enough time so you can settle into your meditation and enjoy the experience. I would suggest that initially you allow yourself thirty minutes to practice the various steps. Spend as much time as you like in your attunement with the Divine. There is no reason to rush through it.

If you are someone who absolutely cannot sit still, or has a deep-seated aversion to meditation, don't give up. Instead, buy or borrow Victor Davich's book *8 Minute Meditation: Quiet Your Mind. Change Your Life*, and commit yourself to his recommended practice. You will soon find yourself hungering for meditation.

Meditation Posture

Meditating in a chair with a firm seat and a fairly straight back works best, because it allows your body to stay most comfortable, even during a long meditation. It also promotes an energy flow that is most conducive to spirit communication. Sit upright and put both feet on the floor, legs uncrossed. Let your hands relax in your lap, palms facing upward and open to receive. I do not recommend meditating in the prone position, because you are more likely to fall asleep than to successfully meditate.

Opening Prayer

As in my other spiritual work, I open my daily meditation with an invocation. I recommend that you do the same. Please note that I do not ask to be connected to spirit guides or deceased loved ones during my morning meditation. I simply reach out to the Great Mystery. I like to use the following prayer:

"Infinite Spirit, Great Mystery; thank you for this beautiful day and for this opportunity to commune with you. I have missed you, and I long for your Divine Presence. Please join me in my meditation. Surround me with your love and light. Please share your wisdom and your teachings with me. Let me be what you would have me be, so that I may serve you. Amen."

Basic Meditation

I listed the elements of a basic meditation that I have found to be helpful for anyone, including those who have no prior experience with meditation. This meditation works whether you are meditating alone or with others.

You might want to create an audio recording of these guided meditations so you can listen to them. Be sure to go slowly, and pause for a few seconds between each sentence, and longer between paragraphs. Give yourself plenty of time to concentrate on each step. I have broken the meditation down into three steps. Each one builds upon the previous one, so take your time to become proficient with each step before you move on to the next one.

Step 1: Relaxing the Body

Close your eyes. Take a couple of nice, deep, cleansing breaths. Inhale all the way into your abdomen, and gently release. Adjust your posture, so that you are comfortable. Begin to relax your brain and your mind. Let thoughts drift away like clouds on a sunny day, becoming peaceful and serene; let go of all expectations. Let all external sounds in your environment take you to a deeper level of calm and relaxation.

Begin to relax your feet. Release all tension in your toes, ankles, shins, and calves. Relax your knees and thighs, buttocks, and abdomen. Relax your lower back and your tummy. Relax your lower back and your chest. Relax your upper back. Let go of all tightness in your shoulders and in the back of your neck. Let the relaxation expand down into your arms and hands. Relax your wrists and fingers. Relax your throat, mouth, and tongue. Relax your ears. Soften your face and the tiny muscles around your eyes. Unfurl your forehead and your scalp. Each breath becomes more peaceful, relaxed, and calm.

Step 2: Centering

Now bring your awareness to your spiritual center inside your body. You might locate this center in your heart center in the middle of your chest. Or perhaps you feel this spiritual center in your belly or in your head. Take your time to experiment and learn where you feel most balanced, most centered. Feel your energy gather in this special place and notice how you are beginning to feel more vibrant and alert.

Step 3: Focusing on the Breath

Now gently focus your attention on your breath. Feel your chest expand as you inhale. Notice how the air gently leaves your lungs and how your chest falls as you exhale. Breathing in again, feel the expansion of your chest and exhale, unwinding your mind.

With each inhalation let your heart center, that loving, caring place in the center of your chest, expand and become softer and more loving. As you exhale, breathe out love. Notice how your love radiates through the universe. Take another breath.

Notice the air flowing through your nostrils, down your windpipe, and into your lungs, gently expanding your lungs, chest, and abdomen, filling your heart with a wonderful energy. Gently exhale, letting go of all emotions and energies that no longer serve you, going into deeper and deeper relaxation as your chest rises and falls: rising as you breathe in, falling as you breathe out, like waves rolling in and out. Thoughts come and thoughts go; just let them go, and continue to focus on your breath.

Meditation to Facilitate Spirit Communication

Once you have become familiar and comfortable with the basic meditation, you will be ready to add two additional steps that are fundamental to your ability to connect with spirits. Step 4 and step 5 will help you achieve a perfect balance and harmony between yourself, Mother Earth, and Infinite Intelligence. Over time, this balance helps you become a clear conduit for spirit communication. *Please note that you are not yet seeking to connect with spirits.*

Step 4: Blend Earth and Divine Energy

Once you are relaxed and your mind is calm, take a few moments to greet Mother Earth and thank her for all her blessings. Next, imagine you have little roots attached to the bottoms of your feet. Imagine these roots extend all the way into Mother Earth.

With the next breath, draw up the earth energy through the bottoms of your feet, just as a tree drinks up the moisture of the soil through its roots. Let the earth energy flow up your legs, through your thighs, and into your body.

Next, reach up through the top of your head to the divine presence. Let the divine energies descend upon you, enveloping you in a bubble of love and light. Let the divine energies flow into your body through the top of your head, blending with the earth energies.

Step 5: Attunement with the Divine

Become aware of the eternal spark within you, that divine spark that animates you and gives you life. Let the divine spark ignite your chest into the magnificent flame of the God presence within you. Gently notice how your chest rises and falls with each breath.

Now let the divine flame within you merge with the Divine Presence all around you. Bring yourself into attunement, into alignment with the Divine Presence. Just as an instrument is tuned to the sound of a tuning fork, attune yourself to the presence of the Divine. You instinctively know how to do this: It is as natural as breathing, because you are part of God. Nothing is more natural than to come into harmony with the Divine.

Spend as much time as you like enjoying your communion with the Great Mystery. Do not rush this process. Let divine love enfold you, and fill you, and surround you, touching your heart and your soul.

Never skip your attunement with the Divine, whether you are meditating by yourself or in a group. I cannot overemphasize the importance of this step; spiritual phenomena and spirit communication flow from this process.

This process is also beneficial for all aspects of your life. If you seek your attunement with the Great Spirit on a daily basis, you will come to realize that your life begins to run more smoothly, that you will begin to choose your battles more wisely, that you have much greater compassion for other people as well as for yourself.

Additional Tools

People often complain about how hard it is to stay focused during meditation. Their minds are like small children, drawing attention to all sorts of distractions no matter how much they want to relax. If this describes your experience, you may occasionally wish to add the following exercises to your meditation. Used regularly, these exercises will help you hold your focus for longer stretches of time.

Exercise: Counting Backward

Once your body is relaxed, continue to breathe slowly and evenly. Begin to count backward from one hundred. Really see or imagine the number in your mind in nice, big, bold print. See *100…99* (see or imagine 99 in a nice big font)…*98* (envisioning 98)…This sounds easy, but here is the caveat: when you notice that you've lost focus and have started to think about something else, go back to 100 and start again.

Exercise: Chanting Om

Inhale deeply, and as you exhale, chant "Om." You really want to draw out the "Om" sound for as long as you can maintain the exhalation. Really feel it resonate throughout your being. It's a powerful way to clear the mental chatter and connect you with the sacred realms.

Exercise: Incorporate a Mantra to Stay Focused

Silently repeat an affirmation, or a verse from a psalm, prayer, or favorite poem that addresses your favorite distraction. For example, if you find that you are distracted by worries about money during meditation, you might want to repeat: "I am open to abundance." If you find yourself rehashing the argument you had with your spouse or colleague, you might want to counteract the distracting thoughts with, "Love is patient, love is kind," and let the thought go. If you find yourself regretting choices that you've made in the past as you are trying to meditate, repeat: "I took the road less traveled, and that has made all the difference." Keep your mantra short and meaningful.

Questions & Answers

I just can't meditate.

Try giving yourself a three- to five-minute period before meditation where you sit quietly in your meditation chair. Keep your eyes open and let them rest on an item that is deeply meaningful to you, perhaps a crystal, a candle, a feather, or a beautiful plant or bouquet of flowers. Begin to take a few deep breaths and let your mind and body settle down before you begin the meditation process.

I keep getting distracted.
Author Jack Kornfield[4] recommends a technique called naming the distraction. Instead of getting upset that you keep getting distracted, identify the distraction and give it a name: For example, if you are distracted by feeling restless, quietly say to yourself: "Restless. Restless. Restless." Or if you are angry about something, quietly acknowledge: "Angry. Angry. Angry." Naming the distraction creates a space of acceptance. I find that once I name the distraction, it quickly disappears.

I fell asleep! Is there something that could help me stay awake?
Make sure you sit upright during meditation, and be sure you don't have a lot of food in your stomach. A fairly empty stomach makes it easier to stay awake. You might also schedule your meditations for a time of day when you are fairly alert. I find that after exercise and a shower, my body is usually ready to sit still, but there is still enough activity in my system to keep me awake. Finally, try to get enough sleep so your body won't try to usurp your meditation time.

I just can't seem to stop my mind from thinking.
Everyone who meditates encounters distracting thoughts. Don't let this upset you. When you realize you've been distracted, just

---

4   Jack Kornfield, *A Path with Heart: A Guide Through The Perils and Promises of Spiritual Life*, Bantam Books, 1993.

go back to focusing on your breath. With time, you will experience fewer distractions.

I keep going in and out of meditation. I can't stay with it for long.
Going in and out is quite normal. With time, patience, and practice, you will be able to retain deeper levels of awareness for longer periods of time. Meditation is very much like swimming: you come up to take a breath, and then you put your face back in the water. When you get pulled out of meditation, just take the next breath and return to it.

I meditate, but nothing happens!
This is very typical for all of us. Most of the time, our meditations are quiet and uneventful, with a purpose of increasing our connections with the Great Mystery. Although spirit communication might occur during a meditation, this is not the primary purpose of meditation, and should not be expected or sought. Just trust that meditation has a cumulative effect that builds over time. Be patient and keep meditating.

I tell my spirit people to show up in my meditations, but they don't.
Let go of your expectations and the need to control what happens in meditation. Meditating with expectations is very much like watching that proverbial pot come to a boil: it is a miserable experience. Let go of your need to have a specific goal for your meditations. By having a goal, you set yourself up for a challenge. Spirit communication develops at its own pace. As mediums we

really cannot force our development. The best we can do is to get out of our way and trust that everything is as it should be.

I have been meditating for weeks, but
I'm not sure that I get anything out of it.
Then change your approach to meditation. Instead of looking to "get something" out of meditation, approach it with an attitude of giving yourself over to something larger than yourself. Think about what it is that you can bring to meditation. What can you give to your time with the Great Spirit?

Perhaps what you can give to meditation is your discipline. Perhaps it is your patience and your trust. Perhaps you can bring a loving heart. Perhaps what you bring is your prayer for the well-being of all life. Perhaps your gift to meditation is a desire to be a light in the world, intending and trusting that by sitting in silence you contribute to peace and harmony on the planet. My students usually find that once they focus on giving instead of taking, their struggle with meditation disappears.

Why do I need to meditate when I already
experience spontaneous spirit contact?
Regular meditation creates a permanent change in your vibration as it draws you closer to the Divine Presence. Meditation makes us more sensitive to the presence of high-level spirit beings and enables us to practice high-quality mediumship. If you want to progress beyond your current level of mediumship, a meditation practice is essential.

5

The Spiritual Senses

Mediums experience the presence of the spirit people subjectively through the spiritual senses. The spiritual senses function very much like our physical senses do, except they pick up the higher and finer vibrations of the spirit world. The spiritual senses are referred to with the prefix "clair-." We thus have clairvoyance, clairaudience, clairsentience, claircognizance, clairolfaction, and clairgustation.

The most important difference between the physical senses and the spiritual senses is the fact that in the physical world all our senses function simultaneously: we can see the kitchen, hear and smell the bacon sizzling in the skillet, and sense our teenager's impatience to get out the door without wanting to wait for breakfast. The spiritual senses, however, tend to work laterally; only one piece of information comes in at a time. In other words, mediumship is not like going to the movies, where all the medium has to do is kick back with a bag of popcorn!

Most mediums notice that one or two spiritual senses are usually predominant. It is rare to find a medium who has full access to all the spiritual senses at the same period in life.

When I began to commit myself to the development of my mediumship, I was mainly clairaudient and somewhat clairvoyant. With time my clairvoyance developed to the point that it is now much stronger than my clairaudience. During the last several years, my clairsentience has developed, as well. One of my friends was naturally clairsentient. Over the course of four or five years, his clairvoyance and clairaudience began to kick in and are now almost as strong as his clairsentience.

To help you develop your ability to perceive the spirit people, I am including a number of exercises for each of the spiritual senses. While it is natural to rely heavily on your strongest clair, I urge you to regularly practice the exercises for your less-developed senses. Consider the physical senses; someone who has a weak eye muscle has to tape the good eye shut to make the weak one work twice as hard so it will become stronger.

Please know that there is no way to fail at any of the exercises. Please be patient with yourself, especially if you are doing an exercise for one of your non-dominant senses. It could take multiple attempts during the course of several weeks before you begin to receive impressions for a given exercise. Just as human beings first have to learn to crawl and walk before they can run or dance, development of our spiritual gifts also takes time. You wouldn't expect to play the guitar like musician Carlos Santana after your first guitar lesson, so you probably won't perceive Spirit the way medium John Edward does. Remember, this is new for you. Continued practice, though, brings mastery.

And remember: you often learn more through your mistakes than by getting things right the first time. At the end of an exercise, you might realize you were receiving the information correctly, but that your analytical mind talked you out of it.

The mystic poet Rumi once said that beyond the idea of right and wrong, there is a field; he'll meet us there. Please approach the exercises with Rumi's attitude. Let go of judgment—including self-judgment—and just have fun.

Clairvoyance

Clairvoyance means "clear seeing" or "soul seeing." Clairvoyance is defined as the ability to receive visual impulses such as pictures, symbols, or images that are sent by spirit communicators.

If you are clairvoyant, you will see images through your mind's eye without the aid of your physical eyes. Clairvoyance often feels similar to daydreaming or as if your imagination is making up pictures as you visualize various situations and scenarios. Occasionally, I meet a beginning medium who mistakenly thinks that clairvoyant pictures will appear on the back of her eyelids and that she must look there with her physical eyes. I don't know who perpetuates that myth, but it is simply *not* true!

Beginning mediums assume that clairvoyance is the cat's meow of mediumship, but it is simply one of the easiest to understand. That's because sight is arguably the most important sense in the physical realm; it keeps us from bumping our heads, falling down the stairs, and running into passing cars, and it alerts us to the mugger lurking in the shadow as we pull into our driveway at night.

In mediumship, however, clairvoyance isn't nearly as important as vision is in the physical realm. There are plenty of excellent mediums who are not clairvoyant at all, but they receive wonderful proof of the continuity of life through one or more of the other spiritual senses.

At the same time, even for the most sensitive clairvoyants, only snippets—bits and pieces of information—are seen at one time. If we expand on the movie metaphor, a clairvoyant episode might provide just a couple of visuals—perhaps an image of a particular person, or a place, or someone picking up an object—as opposed to a complete, coherent story. It would make spirit communication so much easier if "the whole show" just appeared before our eyes. Perhaps the misconception of a medium being able to see the whole story in one go has come from our attempts to convey clairvoyant experiences in the media.

Another misconception is that clairvoyance manifests as a rapid succession of images in your mind's eye. That's the way Hollywood directors portray mediumship, because they need a visual cue to let viewers know that their subject is a medium. In reality, I have never known anyone who experiences clairvoyance in that way. Recognizing what to expect is essential, because occasionally beginning mediums dismiss very valid visual information because they are waiting for full cinematic effects.

Let's consider a common example of clairvoyance: you are visiting a friend and suddenly see with your inner vision that an older woman is standing next to your friend. She looks to be in her mid-sixties, heavyset, and of average height. You might not be able to perceive her facial features. When you ask her to come into sharper focus, you notice almond-shaped blue eyes and a heart-shaped face.

As you describe your impressions to your friend, you might notice you can suddenly perceive the spirit woman's attire more clearly. She is dressed to the nines in a plush mink coat and nice shoes, and she's holding something in her hand, though you can't quite determine whether it is a newspaper or a handkerchief—or, wait, is that a theater program?

Now, if your clairvoyance is just beginning, you might only be able to perceive the shape of the lady and not all of the details. The ability to perceive details is something that develops with time and practice.

If you are clairvoyant, you have to train yourself to be very observant so you can notice and describe whatever details you perceive in your mind's eye, because this is the information the sitter requires. You are the sitter's eyes. Your ability to observe minute details is a matter of practice and discipline. Spirit will not necessarily highlight each distinctive feature, but will count on the medium to pay close attention.

Meanings behind what is clairvoyantly presented are difficult to determine. In the example of the woman standing beside your friend, you would not be able to tell from the vision alone what the relationship was between this woman and your friend, why she is visiting her at this time, or the significance of her attire. You wouldn't know if the visitor was happy or what regrets she might have about how she lived her life. Clairvoyance tells only part of a story—a story that likely will be filled in with information conveyed in another way. That's why primarily clairvoyant mediums must also pay attention to what they perceive through the other spiritual senses. Then the sitter can receive as complete a picture as possible, so as to ask questions or make conclusions about the spirit person's visit.

Clairvoyance Exercises

Exercise: People-Watching through the Compassionate Heart

One very simple way of sharpening our spiritual perception is to become more observant in the physical realm. The next time you are stuck in a line at the grocery store or waiting for a friend to arrive at Starbucks, instead of checking your emails or texting on your iPhone, look around and observe the people in your environment with a compassionate heart. The compassionate heart is important, because it will also give you an emotional understanding of the people you'll see. When we look at people without that sense of compassion, it is too easy to fall into the trap of judgment and comparison. When we start judging and comparing, we lose the loving and open mind that is the foundation for all spiritual work.

Pay close attention to how people look. Notice the lines on their faces, their eye color, hairstyles, makeup, clothing, and possible physical ailments. How do they walk? How do they carry themselves? What does their posture tell you about them? You will be able to apply what you learn from observing people in the physical realm to your perception of people in the spirit realm.

Exercise: Picturing the Face of a Loved One in Your Mind's Eye

Clairvoyance works through your imagination, so when you strengthen your ability to visualize people in your mind's eye or "imagine" what they look like, you nourish your clairvoyance.

Close your eyes. Begin to think about a person or pet who is still in the physical realm and who is very dear to you. Imagine looking into your loved one's face. What do this person's features look like? Envision looking into your loved one's eyes. What color are they, and what do they look like when he or she smiles? How does the nose appear? What shape is the forehead? How do his or her lips curl when he or she is happy? What do they look like when he or she is disappointed? Record your observations in your journal. The next time you meet this person, look at him or her and compare how your recollections differed from reality.

Exercise: Sending and Receiving Visual Images

This exercise is wonderful for fostering telepathy, clairvoyance, and providing insight into how we receive visual information from the spirit side of life. A friend and I used to do this exercise about once or twice a week through a period of about six months. It really kicked our clairvoyance into overdrive!

For starters, it is probably best if the two of you agree on what kind of images you are going to be working with. Simple playing cards, clairvoyance cards, or angel cards are wonderful to use in this exercise. Because my friend and I both had several decks of tarot cards, we agreed that we would send each other the image of a tarot card, but we did not specify what kind of deck we would use.

Choose a day and time of day that is mutually agreeable. Decide who is going to go first with sending or receiving an image. At the appointed time, both of you go into meditation at your separate homes, seek your attunement with the Great Mystery, and invite your spirit guides to assist. Once you are relaxed, the sender will look at the chosen card and focus on sending a strong visual image to the receiver. To avoid confusion, make sure the sender only sends the visual image and not the idea or concept or feeling of the card. The receiver will just stay relaxed and open to receiving the image that is being transmitted.

Please note: You are not trying to guess the image or card! You also do not need to be able to identify the Ten of Cups, the Hierophant, or the Eight of Diamonds. It's great if you can identify the card, but making this a requirement could just set you up for failure if you are even slightly off. It is more important to get a good visual image of shapes or color schemes on the card. Also, you may find that you don't see what is on the card at all, but you might instead see people or characters enact the concept of the image.

Afterward, at a prearranged time, call each other and share your experience.

Clairaudience

Clairaudience means "clear hearing" or "soul hearing." Clairaudience is the ability to hear the voices, sounds, and messages from the spirit world with the inner, spiritual ear. Clairaudient people often have extra-sensitive hearing in the physical realm as well and tend to have a hard time putting up with noise. Many musicians are clairaudient, such as Mozart, who was famous for his clairaudience. He usually heard music in his head and then sat down to write down the notes of the music he was hearing. This, no doubt, accounted for how quickly he was able to compose.

Clairaudience is often subtle, fast, and easy to miss. It might seem as if we are talking to ourselves. It can be similar to when we get a song stuck in our heads, where certain words or phrases repeat. Yet clairaudience can also be unmistakably loud and clear.

Spirit warnings to protect us of bodily harm are unmistakable and are often heard clairaudiently.

My most powerful encounter with clairaudience occurred several years ago. I was stuck in a line of cars at a traffic light on Sligo Creek Parkway, approaching Piney Branch Road in Silver Spring, Maryland. Mine was the first car in line, and so I was waiting expectantly for the light to change to green. As I pulled to a stop, I strongly heard a voice in my left ear: "When the light turns green, slowly count to four before you pull out." When the light changed, I did just that: "One...two...three..." I was just about to say, "Four," when a car came flying through the intersection from the left, racing downhill, careening around a curve in the road, and running the red light going at least 60 miles per hour! If I hadn't heeded that message, someone could have gotten killed.

One of my friends recalls how some years ago he was driving in the left lane on the beltway and suddenly a loud and firm voice told him, "Move over." As soon as he switched lanes, traffic in the left lane came to a screeching halt. Had he stayed there, he was sure he would have run into the car ahead of him.

Clairaudience is not necessarily confined to human voices or music. One of my students has the uncanny ability to tell if a used car has been involved in an accident. If so, she hears the sound of breaking glass and metal slamming together.

If you are clairaudient, you might be able to tell whether a spirit visitor had a very deep, husky voice, perhaps with a New York accent. You might be able to hear that she had a smoker's cough. Or you might find yourself thinking about your favorite aria from Puccini's *La Bohème*.

If you experience only clairaudience, you would be able to tell that the woman was an elderly New Yorker with a deep and husky voice who had a smoking-related illness. You would also know that a certain aria from *La Bohème* had special meaning for her. You might infer from this that she was a cultured person. Unless she specifically told you her identity and how tall she was and what she looked like, you would have no idea as to her appearance, economic means, or her relationship to the sitter.

Clairaudience Exercises

It is difficult to develop clairaudience while we are bombarded with sound in the physical realm. You will develop clairaudience more easily if you regularly spend time in quiet surroundings. In other words, get out of the habit of having the radio, television, or stereo creating a constant stream of background noise.

Exercise: Listen to the Sounds of Nature

Make time to head out of the urban environment and into the country or a national park. Being in nature is the most healing thing you can do for yourself. Nature grounds us, and at the same times it opens our awareness to a higher dimension. Spending time in nature and simply listening is also the key that opens doors to clairaudience.

Go to a quiet place in nature where you can sit comfortably and undisturbed for at least fifteen to twenty minutes. This exercise will be especially wonderful if you can find a tree to sit under. Lean your back against the tree for support...close your eyes...breathe deeply...relax...seek your attunement with the Great Mystery...now listen to the sounds of the natural world...listen to the buzzing of insects...notice the chirping of birds both near and far...listen to the wind rustling in the tree branches and the squirrels rustling last year's leaves.

With repeated practice, seemingly magical things begin to happen. You might suddenly "hear" the tree you are leaning against talking to you. You might realize that you can understand what the birds are saying, and you'll even come to understand the messages that come with the wind. You might hear the teachings of rocks. The natural world is full of wise teachers in nonhuman form.

This simple exercise has helped me become more sensitive to the needs of my houseplants. I used to have a brown thumb instead of a green thumb, chronically overwatering or underwatering. By using my mind or observational skills, I never really discovered the balanced middle ground where my plants would be happy. Nowadays, however—after long ago releasing the need to "figure out" what the plants need—I just tune in to them. Now they just ask me for water when they need it. If I forget to tune in, I often hear a polite voice coming from the plants, informing me of their needs, just as my cat touches my foot with a paw to remind me about food or to ask for some attention. Fortunately my plants now thrive, even in the dead of winter!

Once you have done this exercise a number of times and have mastered the art of listening, expand it by adding clairsentience (see *Practice Clairsentience with Trees*).

Exercise: Listen Carefully to Music and Try to Identify the Individual Instruments

Listen to a piece of instrumental music. It doesn't matter whether it is one of your favorites or just one that is playing on the radio, perhaps on the classical music station. Pay attention to the individual notes and to the sound of the individual instruments. Even if you can't name the different instruments, pick one and try to "track" its sound. Notice when other instruments are introduced.

If you have the opportunity to attend the opera or a classical music performance, pay close attention to the timing and the sound of the various instruments. During the tune-up period before a performance, pick out a musician and try to hear that particular person's instrument. When we focus on identifying specific sounds from among a group of sounds, we become better at distinguishing individual voices—and therefore more sensitive to the gentle sounds from the spirit world.

Exercise: Broaden Your Musical Listening Range

Listen to music from decades ago, like that of Ella Fitzgerald, Louis Armstrong, Frank Sinatra, or Edith Piaf. Become familiar with musicals and genres of music that you know nothing about. Music strikes such a deep chord and can convey so much that spirit people often bring their favorite songs into a reading. I have never had a client who wasn't deeply touched when a spirit relative brought a song. When you branch out in what you listen to, you will receive more clairaudient messages simply because you are more familiar with the texture of past eras.

Exercise: Exchange Telepathic "Verbal" Messages with a Friend Across a Distance

This exercise works bests when it is conducted over a series of days. Agree with a friend that during the period of a week the two of you will telepathically send each other one or two strong messages. As you send the messages telepathically, you should also speak the message aloud. I would suggest spending about three to five minutes per message. You might want to send the messages several times during the day. You can do this at random times, like when you are stuck at a red light or in a grocery store line.

There are several ways for you to pick up the messages that your friend has sent to you. For example, you might notice that information just comes to you as you go about your day. Or you might receive the messages during your meditation, or perhaps as you drift off to sleep at night. Pay attention to how you receive the message: do you hear the message with your friend's voice, or is it an inner voice that repeats the message to you?

Clairsentience

Clairsentience means "clear feeling" or "clear sensing." Clairsentience is a medium's ability to receive physical and emotional sensations projected by spirit people. Since people who are clairsentient can actually *feel* the emotions of others, they often interpret their sensitivity as a curse, especially when they feel bombarded by the negative emotions of others. For a medium, though, clairsentience is a wonderful gift. With proper development, a clairsentient medium is able to determine a lot of evidential information about their spirit communicators.

Spirit people often transmit the sensations of the physical ailments they had in life as clues for the living. This means that mediums often feel conditions of the spirit communicators in their own bodies. A sudden burning sensation in your stomach can mean that the spirit visitor used to suffer from acid indigestion or was prone to ulcers. If you are feeling a sudden, splitting headache, you could be connecting with a spirit person who had a stroke or was prone to migraines, or at some point suffered blunt trauma to the head. If you suddenly become aware of pain in your hips, you are probably dealing with a spirit communicator who broke a hip or had a hip replacement during life on Earth.

When I encounter a spirit communicator who suffered from emphysema, smoker's cough, or pneumonia, I always experience the sensation of a sudden mass of mucus in my chest. These sensations can feel so real that you could wonder if you are coming down with something.

As a clairsentient medium, I can also feel medical procedures that the spirit people endured during their lifetimes. When I feel my blood churning, it could be a sign that the person had to undergo dialysis. When I feel the stabbing of needles, I could be dealing with someone who was diabetic and had to inject insulin. A sharp discomfort in my throat usually refers to a feeding tube.

Please note, though, that the physical ailments spirit people bring are *memories* of how their bodies felt to them during certain phases of their life. All physical pain ceases at the time of physical death. The spirit people bring these physical sensations solely for identification purposes so that their relatives on Earth will know beyond a doubt that it really is the spirit entity that is communicating—not because they are still suffering!

The spirit communicators certainly don't mean to torment the medium. In the early days of mediumship development, the physical sensations could feel particularly strong. If they are too much for you, ask your guides to bring you the mini-version, just enough so that you understand what illness or health condition the deceased is talking about, but not so much that you suffer. Once you understand what their problems were, you can also ask them to remove the physical sensations.

Then again, some people welcome strong physical sensations. A friend who attended development classes with me used to ask his guides to make the sensations particularly strong because he thought he was "too dense and insensitive" (his words) to pick up on the subtle spirit vibrations.

I want to point out, though, that clairsentience can be very subtle and barely noticeable. I was reminded of this in a recent morning meditation when my father connected with me. He suffered a debilitating stroke that left him paralyzed on one side. When he connected with me, though, I felt only a very slight sensation of numbness and paralysis on the left side. If I hadn't been sitting in meditation and paying attention, I probably wouldn't have noticed since the sensation was so very light and gentle.

Clairsentient mediums are also able to feel the emotions of the spirit visitors. While you might only wish to experience the mini-version of the physical ailments, you don't want to hold back on feeling their emotions. Many spirit visitors bring tremendous feelings of love for the relatives they've left behind on earth, and you might also be able to feel the regret or sorrow they suffered during various life events. These feelings have meaning and could be very significant to sitters.

Clairsentient mediums are also able to perceive whether a person was male or female, old or young when they passed, how they were related to the sitter, their stature and build in life, whether they were educated, if they were emotionally warm or remote, what their character was like, whether they were honest or dishonest, had a sense of humor, were judgmental or hard-nosed, and dozens of other traits.

Clairsentient mediums often feel a difference in temperature when spirit people are around. Some mediums feel the spirit presence as hot, others as cold. Some only feel a change in temperature in the presence of their spirit guides, others only when they enter the deeper trancelike states of meditation.

Clairsentience Exercises

Exercise: Practice Clairsentience with Trees

This is an exercise that is easily mastered because the tree spirits will eagerly assist you. After you have made your attunement with the Great Spirit, as explained in the *Listen to the Sounds of Nature Exercise*, extend a loving and compassionate heart to your surroundings and begin to pay attention to what you are sensing and feeling. Sense the energy of the tree you are sitting under. Does it feel like a happy tree? Does it feel wise? Does it feel healthy? Does it feel young and vibrant, or does it feel like it is getting on in years?

After you have exhausted the information from one tree, get up and find a different one, perhaps a younger tree or perhaps one that is beginning to die. What does it feel like? Can you sense how it is different from the one you just visited?

Now find a dead tree, perhaps one that has long ago fallen over and is decaying. Sense its lack of life-force energy.

Exercise: People-Watch with Clairsentience

Once you have become proficient at observing people with a compassionate heart, tune in to your clairsentience. As you observe people, pay attention to the physical sensations that come to you. Do you suddenly perceive aches and pains somewhere in your body? If so, you might be picking up on something that is going on with the person you are watching. Also pay attention to your emotions as you watch someone. How does the person feel to you—happy, sad, courageous, open, closed, loving, or angry?

Exercise: Exchanging Feelings with a Friend

This is a great exercise for a home circle or for practicing with someone you know. It even works over the telephone or via Skype. All you will need is a pen and paper to record your impressions. Determine who will go first with sending and receiving. Sit across from each other or the computer screen and have the receiver enter a relaxed, peaceful state. Once the receiver is relaxed, the sender transmits an emotion/feeling to the receiver. For complete novices, the sender should give a clue to the receiver that the feeling is on its way. The sender should concentrate on sending the feeling until the receiver reaches for the notepad. Once the first feeling has been recorded, both sender and receiver should take three cleansing breaths. The sender then begins to send another feeling. After three or four feelings have been sent, switch roles. Compare notes after both of you have served as sender and receiver.

Exercise: Expanding Your Sensitivity and Emotional Vocabulary

The purpose of this exercise is to help you become more attuned to the emotional information that the spirit people might wish to convey. The spirit people will always take the shortest and most direct route in communicating with a medium. They will never tell a long-winded story if they can simply convey what they want to say by sending you a feeling. However, in order to understand the spirit people's emotions, you will need to become aware of how various concepts or ideas feel to you, and you need to develop a vocabulary to describe what you are sensing and feeling. Use any angel card or oracle card deck that you feel connected with.

Get together with a friend. Open the exercise with prayer and then settle into a relaxed, meditative state of awareness. Imagine letting your brain go to mush. Take a deep breath and become aware of your heart center. Have your friend draw a number of angel cards or oracle cards, and ask her to read the concept word that is printed on the card. Let each word or concept drop into your heart center. What does the word feel like? Where in your body do you feel the sensations? Describe what you are sensing and feeling, and have your friend take notes on your descriptions.

Exercise: Clairsentience in Traffic

The next time you go on a road trip, imagine that you have special sensors that extend far beyond your physical body. These sensors allow you to sense the energy of the other drivers. When you become attentive to what you are sensing and feeling in traffic, you can better anticipate the other drivers' next moves. Tune in to the energy of the drivers around you, notice what you sense, and then observe what happens. Can you sense the energy of a distracted driver? How does a cop feel to you when approaching from behind your car? What does it feel like when there is a cop waiting ahead, hoping to catch speeders? You will probably find that you don't even need to look in the rearview mirror to sense the pushy or impatient energy of someone coming up from behind and nearly riding on your bumper.

Once you become proficient at sensing the energy of the other drivers, extend your observations further. Try to sense the reason why the person behind you is riding on your bumper. Is she late to pick up the kids from the babysitter, running late for work, or desperate to get to the airport? Or is the person angry after an argument with a significant other? Are they on the way to the hospital? Initially you might wonder if you are making up what the reasons are, but if you continue practicing, your spirit helpers will give you the opportunity to receive feedback. With time you will become very good at it!

Exercise: Activity with a Group and a Blindfold

Beginning clairsentient mediums often have a hard time telling whether a spirit person is near them. The following exercise is designed to sensitize the clairsentient medium to the feel of the presence of spirit people in the medium's energy field. This is a wonderful exercise to practice in a development circle, especially when there is a mix of gender and age among the participants.

Blindfold one of the circle's participants and have the other participants gather as a group at a distance. Silently select one member of the group to come forward and stand about four feet behind the one who is blindfolded. A facilitator should then coach the person with the blindfold to notice a presence just outside his or her energy field. Invite the other person to approach the blindfolded person until he or she is standing in the energy field of the blindfolded person.

Coach the blindfolded person to notice the feeling of the presence in the energy field. What does it feel like when someone is standing behind you? Also, try to sense if the person behind you is a male energy or a female energy. Does the person feel young or old? Healthy or unhealthy? Happy or sad?

Give the blindfolded person a little bit of time between questions so he or she can tune in to the vibrations of the other person. After a few minutes, have the first person step back and invite another one to come forward. Have one of the observers take notes on the order in which each person stands behind the blindfolded participant.

Once everyone has had a chance to stand behind the blindfolded person, select a new person to be blindfolded and repeat until everyone has had the chance to be blindfolded. Afterward, let people share their experiences.

What I love with this exercise is that people often get creative. A wife might send a hug to her husband as she stands behind him. Another person might send the idea of smoothing the blindfolded person's hair. People who are clairsentient invariably will report feeling the hug or someone smoothing their hair even though the person behind them did not physically touch them.

Claircognizance

Claircognizance means "clear knowing." When we receive extrasensory information that explains ideas and whole concepts, for example, we are experiencing claircognizance. The knowledge is suddenly in our consciousness, coming instantly from out of nowhere, and we can't explain how we know what we know. Claircognizance is often experienced as if our brain has received a full "download" on a subject or situation without our ever having thought of the subject. It is just suddenly there, and we know in every fiber of our being that the information is absolutely correct. And of course, it turns out to be so. People who are mentally oriented often have strong claircognizance. Albert Einstein was famous for suddenly knowing the answer to math and physics problems that he couldn't figure out in his head.

Precognition is a common form of claircognizance, and you don't need to have a PhD in physics in order to be claircognizant. Precognition is knowledge of future events without input from mundane sources of information. Here are a couple of examples of precognition: you meet someone and you suddenly just know things about this person or your future relationship with the person. Later it turns out that things were indeed as you knew they would be. Or perhaps your spouse wants to sell the house you have been living in to purchase a larger one. Even though the purchase price of the new house is only about one-third more than your old house, you just know that the new house will cost you double each month as compared to the one you are living in, though you can't explain why.

Premonition, too, is a form of claircognizance. Premonition differs from simple precognition in that premonition always contains an element of forewarning and danger. I experienced very powerful premonition years ago when my children were small. We had just arrived in Dakar, Senegal, for a week-long vacation. Our flight had been delayed by hours, and we arrived in Dakar at midnight. By the time we exited the airport building, it was 1:20 a.m., and the airport taxi stand was deserted. A couple of young Africans offered to drive us to our hotel, about ninety minutes south of Dakar. My then-husband, who was very familiar with Africa, saw nothing wrong with this offer—and initially I didn't either.

However, when we got to the airport parking lot, I suddenly knew that I was looking at the car my mother had always warned me about getting into. There was nothing wrong with the looks of the car. It was a light-blue Mercedes—in fact, it was in good condition, especially by African standards. There was nothing wrong with the feeling I got from the young men, but I knew we were not supposed to get into that car.

I dug in my heels and insisted, "Let's go back to the taxi stand. One is already on the way. It'll get here in exactly twelve minutes."

Sure enough, twelve minutes later a taxi pulled into the deserted taxi stand and we made our way safely to our destination. How did I know that there was another taxi on the way? I just knew.

I never found out what happened with the blue Mercedes or with the drivers. I have no idea of what would have befallen us had we gone with the young men, but I have never regretted listening to my inner knowing.

A lot of people experience precognition in their dreams. It is not uncommon for people to learn about the imminent death of a loved one through a dream. One of my students always knows when family members will soon die, because she dreams of attending their funerals. Others report dreaming of mass casualties, such as the September 11, 2001, attack on the World Trade Center in New York or the 2004 tsunami that claimed tens of thousands of lives in the South Pacific.

People often ask me why they are given this kind of information in their dreams when there is absolutely nothing they can do to prevent these events.

I believe that we receive this kind of information so that we can intervene—not necessarily with action, but instead with prayer. The spirit people often talk about the big difference prayers made when offered on their behalf. Prayer cushions the blow of whatever is coming, so if you have an unsettling precognitive dream, start to pray for those who will be affected. And if you have a precognitive dream about the passing of a loved one, treat it as heads-up to spend extra time with and to pray for this person.

Claircognizance Exercises

Before we launch into claircognizance exercises, I want to encourage you to not get hung up on whether you've received information through claircognizance alone or perhaps through a combination of clairvoyance and clairsentience. The following exercises are great for helping you develop greater claircognizance, and they might very well improve your clairvoyance and clairsentience, as well.

Exercise: Claircognizance in Your Daily Life

See what you can sense through these simple practices:

+ Before you leave for work in the morning, ask yourself at what time you are going to arrive.

+ When the telephone rings, anticipate who's calling.

+ When you go to the doctor, ask your inner knowing to let you know at what time you'll actually be seen by your doctor.

+ Next time you're stuck at a railroad crossing, ask your inner knowing how many cars are in the train and then begin counting.

+ Next time you are trying to find a parking space in a crowded garage, ask your inner knowing to take you to an empty space.

+ When you go to the post office, ask your inner knowing how many people are going to be in line ahead of you.

When you first start working with these exercises you might feel frustrated if your accuracy is poor. Please don't worry about it—even if you are way off. With time and practice you will definitely get better.

An additional benefit of practicing the claircognizance exercises over the long haul is that you will get really good at sensing how a correct hunch differs from an incorrect hunch. This will help you greatly in distinguishing true spirit communication from your imagination (chapter 8, "Is It Spirit Communication or Imagination?").

Clairolfaction

Clairolfaction means "clear smelling." It is a medium's ability to smell the scent impressions from the spirit world that are not physically present in the room. Some mediums have such fine senses of smell that they can use it to identify illnesses. Spirit people use the path of least effort to make their presence known, so they often use a scent signature to identify themselves. When my grandmother wants to let me know that she is with me, she always brings a strong smell of lavender. Lavender was her favorite scent and she used lavender soaps, lotions, perfume, and sachets.

Please note that spirit scents are not always as pleasant as my grandmother's lavender! My father, for example, loved to eat raw onions. He sometimes brings the smell of raw onions to let me know that he is around, even though it's not exactly my favorite. In a reading, I once connected with a spirit person who had been confined to a nursing home for many years before he died. He presented himself with the acrid smell of urine so typical of nursing homes. The memory of the smell was enough for his granddaughter to recognize him instantly.

Clairolfaction Exercises

The following exercises will help you become more sensitive to and aware of the presence of the spirit people, in part because you force yourself to pay attention to the scent sensations in the physical realm. When we develop our powers of observance in the physical realm, we automatically become more observant of the spiritual realm.

Exercise: Notice the Odors and Scents in the Physical Realm

The most powerful way of developing clairolfaction is to get in the habit of paying attention to smells and fragrances in the physical realm. Here are easy ways to develop this skill.

+ Notice the fragrance of fresh fruit.

+ Pay attention to the smell of desserts. What does a cheesecake smell like? What does key lime pie smell like?

+ Go to a spice store and take time inhaling the different dried herbs and spices.

+ When you go to a restaurant, pay attention to the odors that hit you as you enter. What are the names of dishes that float on the air? What key ingredient(s) can you identify?

+ Go to a garden store and sniff the fragrance of the flowers. Notice the scent of the potting soil. How is the smell of potting soil different from the smell of the soil in your local park?

+ When you go to a friend's house, observe the scent it contains.

+ When you visit an elderly person, notice how this person smells. How does this person's home smell?

+ Notice whether a sick person's odor differs from a healthy person's scent.

+ How is the scent of a baby's skin different from the scent of a grownup's?

+ The next time someone gives you a hug, pay attention to the smell of his or her hair and skin.

+ How does your father's aftershave smell?

+ Go to a cosmetics counter and sample different perfumes. How would you define the fragrance of the different scents?

+ Pay attention to the odor of cleaning materials. How would you describe their scent?

+ Notice the odor of a shoe repair store. How does it differ from the smell of a shoe store?

+ How does the fragrance of one type of rose differ from another?

Describe any odors as you notice them during the day and try to name smells as you notice them.

Exercise: Ask Your Spirit Helpers to Bring You a Fragrance

Once you have become more observant of smells, fragrances, and odors, occasionally ask your spirit guides to join you in a clairolfaction exercise. Ask them to bring you spirit communicators who are willing to share their favorite and unique smell with you. Ask them for a whiff of their favorite perfume or cologne. What did their favorite food smell like? What did their homes smell like?

Clairgustation

Clairgustation means "clear tasting." It is a medium's ability to receive taste and flavor impressions of foods that are projected by the people in the spirit world. Mediums who like to cook and have a broad knowledge of various cuisines and ingredients often have strong clairgustation. The spirit people often remember the foods they used to enjoy while they were still in the physical realm, and during a reading they will bring these taste sensations to the medium. People are always delighted when their spirit loved ones bring the memory of favorite foods, because it's not something they would expect.

Some time ago I had a client whose mother in spirit brought me a very strong taste of Wrigley's Doublemint chewing gum. It turned out that my client's mother often chewed gum, and Wrigley's was her absolute favorite kind. Another spirit visitor brought the taste of her homemade chocolate-chip cookies. She told me she used a secret ingredient in her cookies, and just then I tasted a double dose of vanilla extract. When I mentioned this to my client, she clapped her hands together and burst out laughing! Her relative had *never* shared that secret before—even though family members had asked for it—but the sitter realized the truth as soon as I mentioned it.

Clairgustation Exercises
Exercises: Pay Attention to Taste Sensations in the Physical Realm
Turn off the television, computer, and radio while you eat. Put away the newspaper or the book you are reading and really focus on the taste and textures of the foods you are eating. Try to taste as many individual ingredients as possible. Whenever you eat anything, pay attention to the taste sensations and try to describe them as precisely as possible.

Exercise: Tasting Foods While Blindfolded
This works especially well with a friend who can feed you samples of different foods while you are blindfolded. It's one thing to see a strawberry and to expect the taste

of a strawberry. It's quite different when you don't know whether the bite you are about to take is going to be chocolate mousse, a dill pickle, or beef stroganoff.

Step 6: Notice What You See, Hear, Sense, Feel, Smell, and Taste

Go into your sacred space, settle into your meditation posture, and begin with your opening prayer. Follow steps 1 through 5 in the connecting process.

Continue to relax, focusing on your breath, and continue to send your love to the spirit people. With each breath, the spirit people now come into sharper focus as they begin to make their connection with you. Begin to notice what you sense and feel inside your own body. Notice any physical sensations—perhaps aches and pains—or perhaps muscles the spirit person used often. Notice any feelings and emotions that you are feeling. Perhaps someone is sending love back to you or perhaps you are suddenly thinking of one of your own spirit loved ones. Notice if there are any visual impressions or thought pictures that have drifted into your mind's eye. Pay attention to any sounds that you hear—perhaps in your mind—perhaps in the room that you are sitting in. Notice how a fragrance now comes into your awareness and identify the smell. See if you can smell the scent of cooking and identify any taste you have in your mouth. Gently observe all that is going on in your body and in your awareness. Ask the spirit people to connect with you more closely so that you can better perceive them.

6
Connecting with Spirit: Shifting Your Awareness

Trying to explain how to connect with the spirit world is a little like trying to explain swimming to a nonswimmer: "You get in the water. You lie on your belly. You move your arms and legs in a coordinated fashion so that you can glide through the water." But that's not the essence of swimming. Fluidity in the water depends on intangibles, such as the affinity between swimmer and water, and the swimmer's trust that the water will keep him or her buoyant. The same is true for mediumship.

When mediums connect with the spirit people, they are in an altered state of awareness. So if you want to connect with the spirit people, you will have to learn to shift your awareness out of your ordinary consciousness and into the mediumistic state of consciousness.

Begin by setting an intention that you are going to connect with the spirit world. After you have set your intention, envision flipping an invisible switch located at your temple that opens the door to the spiritual realms. Just switch it "on." Start with an opening prayer to invoke the presence of the Great Mystery and ask for the presence of your spirit helpers and the spirit people. Once you have made your opening prayer, begin to take some deep, relaxing breaths. You should fully expect that a spirit person with something to say will come forward and present himself or herself to your spiritual senses (chapter 5, "The Spiritual Senses").

Most mediums have a trigger that induces a shift in their awareness. For me, the opening prayer is the trigger, and as soon as I close my eyes and start to pray, I perceive a shift in the energy around me. The energy in the room suddenly feels thinner, brighter, and lighter. It feels as if there is a sparkle in the atmosphere that wasn't there before. My personal concerns disappear. Whatever aches, pains, or worries I had before the opening prayer are suddenly gone as I sense the presence of the spirit people surrounding me.

At first I perceive the spirit people as just a faint impression. But as I begin to describe what I sense and feel from the spirit side of life, one spirit person after another comes into sharper focus, and I begin to receive an abundance of information from them through clairvoyance and clairsentience. The mediumistic state of consciousness is unmistakable.

For some mediums the opening prayer alone is not enough to achieve this state. I know several mediums who purposefully empty their minds and hearts of all of their own personal concerns before they can connect with the spirit people. Some people imagine a basket by the door and envision throwing all their earthly concerns into it. Others imagine handing their everyday preoccupations to the Great Mystery for caretaking. A number of my students have told me when they want to connect with the spirit people in my circles, they just "throw their awareness upward, toward the spirit world." In the early days of my development, I often repeated my positive affirmations: "I am Spirit's instrument. I am a conduit for Spirit's love and light. I am open to the presence of the spirit people."

When I give public mediumship demonstrations as part of a religious service, it is not appropriate for me to offer my own individual prayer in front of the congregation. In that case I use a different trigger: I imagine that I am stepping into a sacred circle. As soon as I step into that circle, the connection to the spirit world is there. One of my friends, a fellow medium, says that when he wants to connect with the spirit people in a public forum, he imagines stepping out of his physical body. As soon as he takes the first step, he becomes aware of the spirit people. Some mediums might rub their hands together as the trigger that induces their shift of awareness. Other mediums take a couple of deep, relaxing breaths. I also know mediums who issue a standard greeting to the congregation that helps them make the shift.

As your mediumship unfolds, you will discover your own trigger(s) that gets you to that sweet spot where spirit communication occurs. I suggest you keep your trigger simple. There is no need to invent an elaborate or complicated ritual, because eventually such an exercise would become cumbersome and get in the way of you enjoying your mediumship.

Becoming Aware of the Spirit World

The following practice will help you become aware of your own spirit. Repeat it regularly, because becoming familiar with your spirit will make it much easier for you to detect the presence of spirit people. In the long run it will also help you distinguish between information that comes from the spirit world and thoughts that are generated within your mind (chapter 8, "Is It Spirit Communication or Imagination?").

Read through the entire practice twice, or perhaps create a voice recording of the process to help guide you into a relaxed and meditative state of mind during future sessions.

Practice: Becoming Aware of Your Own Spirit

Turn off the television and silence the telephone. Enter your sacred space and prepare yourself for meditation. Open with a simple prayer along the lines of: "Great Mystery, dear God, surround me with your love and light. Please assist me in becoming aware of and getting to know my own spirit. Thank you. Amen." Close your eyes. Let your breath become deep and even. With each exhalation, release the concerns of your day.

When you are relaxed and peaceful, find the place in your heart where your divine spark resides. Let that divine spark ignite inside you into a beautiful flame. And let that flame burn away anything that is not true and pure. You are now in the presence of your own unique spirit. With each breath, become more aware of your spirit essence. With each breath, let your spirit fill your entire being, and notice how your spirit extends beyond the boundaries of your physical body. Your spirit is limitless, radiant, and infinitely powerful. Spend as much time in this state as you wish. Once your attention returns to the physical realm, say a prayer of gratitude. Record your experience in your journal.

Step 7: Extend Your Awareness Beyond Your Body

You might want to create a recording of the following process or ask a friend to read it out loud to you.

To begin the connecting process, enter your sacred space, assume your meditation posture, and begin to invoke the Divine Presence with an opening prayer. Seek your attunement with the Divine by following steps 1 through 6. Really pay attention to what you are receiving through your spiritual senses.

Imagine that you are an unlimited being who is not confined to the physical body. Extend your awareness to the edge of your physical body and feel your skin as the boundary of your physical being while continuing to breathe deeply. Next, extend your awareness into your energy field—about three to five feet beyond your physical body—in all directions. Notice how your energy field feels to you. You might feel a special tingle or an "electric charge."

When you first begin to work with this step, you might not notice anything special. That's okay. At the very least, this process will give you a good baseline awareness of your energy field and the physical space around you. With time and continued practice, this step will help you notice the presence of the spirit people in your energy field, in the physical space around you, and around other people.

Step 8: Send Love to the Spirit People

With your next exhalation, begin to send love from your heart into your energy field and into the room around you. Send love from your heart to the spirit people who have gathered, regardless of whether you are aware of their presence. Send your love to them anyway, as well as a greeting. You might want to quietly say "hello" and introduce yourself. Continue to send love and continue to breathe deeply.

Exercise: Playing Pretend

As children we had so much fun playing pretend. We pretended to be pirates, princesses, magicians, firefighters, detectives, wizards, and airplane pilots. The moment we decided to pretend, we actually began to impersonate the character we wanted to be. For the duration of the game, we were in an altered state of awareness; we *were* our favorite characters, and as we played, we forgot about our ordinary existence.

In this exercise, get together with a friend or a fellow medium whose deceased family members you know very little about. I want you to "pretend" that you are a medium, that you can connect with your friend's spirit people, and that you can actually impersonate the spirit people. Invite your spirit helpers to help you with this. (You will learn more about your spirit helpers in the next chapter.) Invent each detail about the spirit person just as you would in a game. Just make it up, and have fun doing it. Initially you might not get everything right, but don't worry about that. You are playing a game, and you are having fun. Believe me, it won't take long before your spirit helpers catch on to the fact that when you are playing pretend, you are actually reaching out for the spirit world. Your spirit helpers will make sure there will never be a shortage of spirit people for you to connect with. Eventually, your playing pretend will become very real.

Disconnecting from the Spirit People

It is good practice to conclude each mediumship session with a closing prayer, regardless of whether you are meditating alone at home or participating in a home circle, development circle, or workshop. In the closing prayer, give thanks for your visit with the spirit people and everything they shared with you, even if you didn't receive any impressions.

The closing prayer is the trigger to disconnect. After you have finished the closing prayer, imagine flipping the invisible switch that opens the door to the spirit world to "off." Get up, blow out your candle, and open the windows to let in fresh air. Drinking a glass of water and having a bite to eat will help shift your awareness back into your physical body.

Questions & Answers

I don't notice anything when I extend my awareness beyond my body.
It is okay to not notice anything. There might not be anything special for you to notice at this time. However, you need to know what it feels like when no spirit people are around so that you can actually perceive the very subtle difference when they are present. Also, you must remember that this is new to you and you don't yet have an established frame of reference. Practice extending your awareness beyond the physical realm for at least four months, and you will see results.

It seems silly to play pretend. Isn't it disrespectful to the spirit people?
The spirit world is a lighthearted place. Beginners often think that spirit communication needs to be a very solemn, if not morose, affair. Nothing could be further from the truth. Remember, in order to connect with the spirit world you have to raise your vibration. In other words, you need to find that lighthearted, playful place inside your heart. Playing pretend helps you recover your playful inner child. It raises your energy, and it will help you connect.

7

Spirit Guides and Helpers

One of the joys of being a medium is the privilege of working with spirit guides. Spirit guides are the unseen helpers in the spirit world who are dedicated to working with humanity in many different ways. All of us—regardless of whether we are psychic or spiritual—have spirit guides who help us with our lives, life lessons, and spiritual growth. Spirit guides are often referred to as guardian angels. Many people sense that a loving, caring being watches over them and protects them in potentially life-threatening situations. This sense very likely emanates from the presence of spirit guides, even for people who don't believe in ghosts. Our spirit guides assist us whether or not we are aware of them.

If you want to develop your mediumship to the highest degree, I highly recommend working in collaboration with your spirit guides. They will supervise your development, guide you to the best teachers, and ensure that only the best-intentioned spirit visitors will come to you during meditation and mediumship practice.

There are two general categories of spirit guides: long-term spirit guides and situational spirit guides. From the perspective of developing your mediumship, your long-term guides would be of greatest importance. Situational guides, though, can provide wonderful specialized knowledge in any area of need as the occasion requires.

Long-Term Spirit Guides

Long-term guides are more highly evolved spiritual beings who have dedicated themselves to working with humanity. They know your life purpose and help keep you on track. They guide us and protect us. They also ensure that we are going to meet up with the right people and opportunities to move us along our path. They help open certain doors for us, but also make sure that some doors stay closed so we won't stray too far.

Some of them have been with you since childhood. Others are drawn to you through the Law of Attraction, which states that like attracts like. As you grow spiritually, you will attract guides of a higher vibration.

All of us have a number of guides who work with us on a regular basis. Some play more prominent roles than others. It is not necessary for you to know your guides, and these guides are not necessarily individuals you have known in this physical life. The spirit helpers who are most relevant to your life will introduce themselves when they feel the time is appropriate and you are ready. I assure you that if you have a sincere desire to get to know your spirit guides, you will.

The most important spirit guides for mediums are: master teachers; gatekeepers; healing guides, such as chemists and spirit physicians; and spirit companions. Please realize that the division of labor implied by these names is a Euro-Western construct that our spirit helpers don't necessarily subscribe to. I have to tell you straight off that spirit guide job descriptions are not as narrowly defined as those of the federal government. In fact, skillful guides are able to assume a broad variety of functions.

Master Teachers

Master teachers often focus on disseminating new knowledge, like White Eagle, who was channeled by the medium Grace Cooke, or Silver Birch, who spoke through British medium Maurice Barbanell. They care about humanity's spiritual evolution and our cooperation with others. Their teachings always reflect this broader orientation.

Master teachers often work with many people at the same time. As you progress on your spiritual path, you could be brought into relationships with other spiritual people who share the same master teacher. As individuals, your life purposes, gifts, and talents may differ, but you probably share a common higher mission and were brought together for that purpose.

Master teachers are generally not particularly interested in the details of our lives. They bring us our life lessons, and they tend to show us how we fit into the big picture. They invariably challenge us to stretch beyond personal self-interest and to serve a higher spiritual purpose.

These guides often have a particularly high vibration. Beginning mediums can find it difficult to get in touch with master teachers, as these helpers can feel very distant and remote. Initially, you will probably find it much easier to communicate with one of your personal spirit guides instead of with your master teacher, even though your master teacher is still working with and through you.

We don't get to choose our master teachers, though. They seek out those on the physical plane with whom they want to work. However, if we wish to attract a high-level master teacher, it helps if we make ourselves spiritually attractive. This involves living in alignment with natural law and trying to be the most conscientious and ethical person possible.

Gatekeepers

Gatekeepers can be compared to the marines who guard American embassies. They guard the access between the spirit world and the physical realm. If a medium desires contact with a person's spirit loved one, the medium's gatekeeper will send word to others who then find this person in the spirit world and bring him or her into contact with the medium.

Every medium has gatekeepers who control the spirit people who are permitted around the medium. Gatekeepers also ensure the spirit people who come into a reading are willing to provide the evidential information the medium requires. They also keep order in a reading or in a public demonstration, ensuring only one person speaks at a time so that a reading won't turn into chaos.

Gatekeepers also take a leading role in spirit rescue. They help put us in touch with troubled spirits who are ready to accept our help in their struggle to move on with their path in the spirit world. In spirit rescue, the gatekeeper coordinates with the troubled spirit person's guides and departed loved ones to facilitate escort to the higher realms.

We often have the same gatekeeper over long stretches of time until the gatekeeper feels that it is time for him or her to move on to other occupations or responsibilities in the spirit world. In such a situation, the medium's other spirit guides coordinate the replacement with a new gatekeeper.

I occasionally visit my gatekeeper using process one, "Meet a Spirit Guide." During these visits, I like to thank him for all the help that he is providing. If there has been a change in gatekeepers, I like to brief the new gatekeeper with the kind of information that I would like the spirit people to provide me with in my readings (chapter 11, "Evidence and Spirit Messages").

Healing Guides

In the old Spiritualist writings, healing guides were often referred to as spirit doctors or spirit physicians. Spirit doctors are important to those who have a connection to the medical profession or who have the gift of healing mediumship. Spiritualist forerunner Andrew Jackson Davis, twentieth-century medical clairvoyant

Edgar Cayce, and Brazilian healer John of God are examples of healing mediums with particularly skillful spirit physicians. Reiki teachers and practitioners, for example, work with the Reiki healing guides, including Mikao Usui, Dr. Chujiro Hayashi, and Hawayo Takata, who introduced the Reiki healing system to the Western world.

All of us have healing guides, even though we may not be involved in the medical profession or in healing mediumship. We can turn to them for help with our own health and healing issues. Whenever I face a health crisis, in addition to seeking proper medical care, I always turn to my healing guides and ask them to take the illness away. Thanks to their assistance, I have made amazing and rapid recoveries from pesky illnesses like the flu and shingles. I credit the help of my healing spirit helpers for the fact that I rarely get the common cold.

Spirit Companion

You might have one spirit helper who is closer to you and with whom you have a deep emotional affinity. This is your spirit companion, though he or she often fulfills other roles as well. I know that my spirit companion works with me in my mediumship. He often teaches through me, and I feel that he is in charge of who is allowed in the séance room.

Your spirit companion is often similar to you in some ways. There could even be similarities between your life struggles and the struggles that your spirit companion faced while on earth.

During life's ups and downs, our spirit companions are wonderful sources of comfort. The spirit companion might not be a master teacher and might be reluctant to advise you on matters that are better addressed by your master teacher. However, a few words from him or her can give us the strength to keep on going. Knowing that they have struggled with the same challenges that we face can help us immeasurably in making it through a rough patch.

Situational Spirit Guides and Spirit Experts

Situational spirit guides, as the name implies, are spirit helpers who are with us for a short time to help us with specific tasks. Situational guides do not need to be highly evolved spiritual masters in order to assist us, and therefore can be recent arrivals to the spirit world. Their expertise in a given subject—the subject on which they are consulting for you—was acquired during their lifetimes on earth. Situational guides are wonderful resources, and all we have to do is ask for their assistance. When a particular task is completed, a situational guide moves on to the next challenge.

When I was studying the Morris Pratt Institute course on modern spiritualism to become an NSAC-certified medium, teacher, and ordained minister, a white-haired spirit gentleman with big wireframe glasses who asked me to call him Joe often helped me with my lesson essays. I could tell by the depth of Joe's knowledge that he was an old Spiritualist, but without knowing more than the first name Joe, I wasn't sure exactly who he was, although it didn't really matter. I was about halfway through the course when I attended a seminar at Lakeside Assembly Hall in Lily Dale, New York, and found a photograph of my spirit helper hanging on the wall. I instantly recognized him. He looked exactly as he had appeared to me. It turns out Joe was late NSAC President Joseph Merrill! When I shared this with a friend who knew Joe during his lifetime, my friend laughed and said, "Of course, he told you to call him Joe. He told everyone to call him Joe!"

In the years since I have concluded my studies and have become certified and ordained, I have only had occasional contact with Joe, specifically when I was writing lectures and sermons on Spiritualism. No doubt, he helps all the students of Spiritualism from the other side.

My most recent experience with a situational spirit helper was when I needed help with search engine optimization for my website. An optimization company had contacted me and offered its services for a continuing monthly fee equivalent to a car payment. I declined, but asked my spirit guides to send me an expert who could help me understand the intricacies of search engine optimization. It took about seven months, but finally Spirit connected me to a search engine optimization specialist in the spirit world who cleared up a lot of my confusion. I'm sure the reason it took so long to find one is that most specialists in this line of work are still young, enjoying life on earth.

We can receive help from a situational guide at any time. If you are a college student studying a challenging subject, ask for a gifted expert teacher on the subject to assist you as you prepare for your exams. Now, you will still have to do your part and study, but the presence of the spirit teacher can help you grasp difficult concepts more readily and can help you understand subject interrelationships.

If your central heating unit stops on a particularly cold day of a three-day holiday weekend when no professional help is available, you can ask for an expert in heating units to help you figure out how to make your heater start up again.

You can also call upon situational helpers to assist you in your interpersonal relationships. For example, if you and your partner are struggling with communication, invite a marriage counselor from the spirit world to be with you when the two of you talk. Ask to be clearly guided so you can conduct your end of the conversation in the most productive way and truly hear your partner's perspective.

To receive the help of a situational guide, simply say a prayer and ask that an expert in the spirit world with specialized knowledge in the area of your need be sent to you. If you have already been working with spirit guides, you may actually be able to perceive a situational guide. But even if you don't, please be assured that the expert is there to help you. When we are working with a situational guide, we usually are guided to take the correct actions in the right order. Or we might just have a sudden knowing on how to proceed in a given situation. And of course, always thank your spirit guides for all their help!

Characteristics of Spirit Guides

Before you decide to fully trust a spirit person who purports to be a guide, be sure to use your discernment to evaluate the guidance that this being brings. The old Spiritualists always encouraged us to test the spirits. This is sage advice. Trust builds gradually, both in earth relationships and Earth-Spirit relationships. Your spirit guides will never hold it against you if you proceed cautiously and request proof. They will be happy to corroborate the information they provide through various avenues.

Sadly, there are spirit people stuck in the lower astral realm. They are known as earthbound spirits. These spirits are not spiritually advanced, and thus they are in no position to help anyone. However, they do get lonely and bored. They often like to feel empowered and important, so they might briefly try to pass themselves off as spirit guides.

If you conduct your spiritual work within the parameters of prayer and if you are not particularly desperate to connect with a spirit guide, this should not be an issue for you. Fortunately, it is easy to distinguish genuine spirit guides from imposters reaching out from the lower astral realm.

Genuine Spirit Guides:

+ Care about you.

+ Have your highest good and life purpose at heart.

+ Are patient, kind, compassionate, loving, and wise.

+ Are true to their word and give wise guidance.

+ Facilitate win-win situations for all involved.

+ Offer empowerment, support, and encouragement.

+ Provide loving insight into other people's perspectives.

+ Offer new perspectives and spiritual insight regarding challenging situations.

+ Help you to see the lessons and teachings that people and situations bring to you.

+ Remind you that you have free will.

+ Insist that you make your own decisions.

+ Might tell you something you don't want to hear, but they do so in a wise and loving manner.

+ Take their time in establishing a relationship with you.

+ Understand that trust builds gradually.

+ Will bring plenty of corroborating evidence that proves they are who they say they are.

+ Will bring you the same message or advice repeatedly.

Genuine Spirit Guides Never:

+ Scheme to hurt another person.

+ Help you punish people who have hurt you.

+ Incite feelings of inadequacy or vengeance.

+ Judge or condemn others.

+ Boost your ego and tell you that you are special.

- Tell you that you are better than others.

- Put you down.

- Criticize you for mistakes you've made.

- Frighten you or appear to you in a frightening manner.

Lower Astral Plane or Earthbound Imposters:

- Often come on like gangbusters.

- Love to make predictions of a disastrous nature.

- Thrive on heightened emotions such as fear, anger, and rage, and strive to inspire such feelings in you.

- Like to stir up bad feelings between people.

- Often have a divide-and-conquer mentality.

- Love to boost your ego by telling you that you are chosen for great deeds, that you are a person of great importance, or that you are going to be rich and famous.

- Have no interest in your spiritual growth.

- Have no interest in helping anyone.

- Might make you feel powerless.

One of my friends told me that her deceased mother had come to her saying she would be my friend's spirit guide. During the following weeks, the purported spirit guide no longer looked or felt like her mother. Instead, she took on a frightening appearance. The "guide" had also taken to waking the person at all hours of the night with all sorts of nonsense that I no longer recall.

I told my friend that this so-called guide was neither her mother nor a spirit guide. In all likelihood this new medium had met up with an earthbound spirit who felt lonely and wanted to mess with her. It took a couple of coaching sessions, but eventually my friend summoned the courage to send this imposter away. The imposter was initially reluctant to leave, but when my friend kept insisting and did not waver, the imposter cleared out and didn't return.

The moral of the story is: if contact with a so-called guide or any spirit person ever makes you feel threatened, uncomfortable, or restricted, tell that entity to leave! Be firm and tell him or her to go to the light. Ask the Great Spirit to send you a higher-level guide to assist you. Just as you don't have to tolerate poor treatment from people in the physical world, you surely don't have to accept it from anyone in the spirit world.

I have never known of a situation where firm insistence on the part of the medium did not work. However, should you ever notice that the same spirit person keeps coming around with the same sad story, realize that you are probably in contact with a spirit person who is stuck and in need of help (appendix A, "Earthbound Spirits and Conducting Spirit Rescue").

Important Things to Keep in Mind

Whether you work with situational guides or long-term guides, it is important that you have a realistic understanding of what to expect when you work with spirit guides.

+ Your relationship with your spirit helpers should be based upon common sense and mutual respect.

+ You have free will and you are responsible for your life at all times. You should never abdicate that responsibility to anyone. Spirit guides can and do provide help and insight, but they cannot live your life for you. They cannot and should not make your decisions for you.

+ Working with spirit guides does not guarantee a smooth ride through life. Reality dictates that we are on Earth to learn and evolve spiritually. Most of us learn only through experience.

+ Working with a spirit guide is no substitute for doing your part. If you are job-hunting, for example, do ask your spirit guides to draw your attention to appropriate positions. After that, however, it is up to you to write the best résumé possible and to prepare yourself for the interview and the position as fully as you can. If you are lackadaisical, don't expect your guides to bail you out.

+ Spirit guides aren't sugar daddies or fairy godmothers that cater to your every whim, making sure you get what you want from life without ever stubbing a toe. They support us on our life path, ensuring that we have what we need to fulfill our life purpose.

+ Spirit guides will not prevent us from getting hurt—
  especially if getting hurt supports our spiritual
  evolution, as it often does. During a tough patch in
  your life, your guides will offer love and support. This
  can literally make the difference between being able to
  bear a situation and just throwing in the towel.

+ Spirit guides might have a very different perspective
  on what is best for you than you do. If you ask them
  about what job is best for you, you might be thinking
  about a job that's easy, gets you fast promotions, and
  provides top pay. Your spirit guides, however, might
  not deem such perks as priorities. They might know
  you need to learn to become a better team player or
  that you need to learn to stand up for yourself. In that
  case you are likely to find yourself in job situations
  that challenge you to develop those missing qualities.

+ Spirit helpers are not infallible. It is true they tend
  to have a better overview of what is going in your life
  than you might have, and are thus able to help. But
  they cannot force things to happen and they cannot
  tell you for certain whether or not something will
  happen. That is because many life situations depend
  on cooperation with others, and these others also
  have free will that they must exercise.

How to Engage Your Spirit Guides in Your Mediumship

Engaging your spirit guides in your mediumship is a simple four-step process. If you engage in this process every time you intend to communicate with the spirit world, then the process will become automatic and second nature.

1. Intend to work with your spirit guide in the development of your mediumship.

2. Before you attempt to connect with the spirit world, tell the spirit people they need to go through your gatekeeper if they want to communicate through you.

3. In your opening prayer, remember to issue an invitation to your spirit guides to join and assist you.

4. When you are ready to meet the spirit people, ask your guides to bring them to you.

Meeting Your Spirit Guides

It is best to attempt to connect with your spirit guides after you have established a spiritual practice based on regular meditation and prayer. If you are a complete novice to all things spiritual, I would suggest you give yourself several months of regular meditation and prayer practice before attempting the two processes below. During these months, it is okay to harbor the heartfelt desire to meet your spirit guides.

The reason I suggest waiting is that initially your vibration might not yet be high enough to connect with your guides, and your spiritual senses might not yet be acute enough to perceive your spirit helpers. I find that many people meet their spirit helpers quite naturally once they begin a regular spiritual practice and start practicing the application of the natural laws.

I met my favorite spirit guide organically some months after I had started a daily meditation practice. One day I simply noticed his presence. He was quiet and had a sweet little smile on his face, but he didn't interact with me. However, I immediately liked him. There was just something very comforting and positive about him, and I felt drawn to him. I realized I had sensed his presence for a while, but I had been simply too busy to slow down and pay attention.

After our initial encounter I began to notice his presence more frequently. Because he didn't say anything to me, I just assumed that he came with the house that I lived in. When I told my Spiritualist friends about him, they just smiled, but they didn't venture any guesses. It never occurred to me that he could be a spirit guide.

When the time came to move out of the house, I was upset. I didn't want to move, partly because I was afraid I wouldn't encounter the spirit gentleman again. Imagine my surprise and joy when he showed up during the home inspection of the new house I was about to move to! That was the first time it began to dawn on me that he might be a spirit helper.

Gradually, he began to share small details of his life with me and help me with various large and small things in my life. However, for years he would not share his name, and he spoke of his ethnic background only in the most general of terms.

About four to five years passed after our initial meeting before he finally shared his identity with me. Once he divulged his identity he brought an abundance of detailed corroborating evidence that left no doubt that he is indeed who he says he is.

Why did it take him so long to do this? I believe it is because he knows that mutual trust grows with time and should not be rushed. There were occasions where I might have turned my back on spirituality and Spiritualism. I also think he wanted to see whether I was serious in my commitment to working with the spirit world. After all, a lot of people dabble a little and give up when they don't achieve the results they want as quickly as they had hoped.

Processes to Help You Meet Your Spirit Guides

Physically prepare yourself and your environment with the intention of performing a sacred spiritual ceremony in which you will meet your spirit guide. Take a shower or bath beforehand and put on fresh, clean clothes. Follow the guidelines for preparing a sacred space outlined in chapter 2, "Creating Sacred Space."

Memorize or record the following processes, or a have friend read them to you to help guide you into meditation.

Process One: Meet a Spirit Guide

Go into a relaxed, meditative state and seek your full attunement with the Divine as outlined in steps 1 through 5. Please do not rush the attunement process in your eagerness to meet a spirit guide. After you've had a thorough and leisurely attunement period, extend your awareness into your energy field (step 6) and begin to send your love to the spirit people around you, as described in steps 7 and 8.

Now that you have enjoyed your communion with the Divine, ask the Great Mystery to take you to a sacred place of initiation, a place that is filled with all the love in the universe. It is in this space that you will meet your highest-vibration spirit guide. Gently notice how all of your senses suddenly become more acute. Spend a few moments adjusting your perception. Feel the love that fills this sacred space. Notice your surroundings: an altar has been prepared in anticipation of your arrival. The light of many candles lights up the altar and your surroundings. A master of ceremonies now comes forward and leads you into the center of a circle where a gathering of high-level spiritual beings begins to surround you.

Your highest-vibration spirit guide welcomes you. Open your heart, and sense and feel the energy signature of your spirit guide. Notice the visual impressions. You may or may not see every detail of your spirit guide's face and appearance. Introduce yourself and wait for a reply. Ask what role this guide is going to play in your life. Ask how he or she will help you develop your mediumship. Ask if there is something your spirit guide would like to say to you and wait for a reply. Ask how you can call upon your spirit guide and receive the answer. When you feel your meeting with your spirit guide is complete, gently return your awareness to your physical surroundings. Wiggle your feet and legs, shake out your hands, and stretch.

Process Two: Thinning the Veils of Separation

This process is wonderful for people who have a hard time working with visualization. It can also be used any time you feel burdened or bogged down with whatever is going on in your life.

Go into a relaxed, meditative state and seek your full attunement with the Divine as outlined in steps 1 through 5.

Once you have attuned yourself to the divine energies, continue to enjoy the peace and calm of your meditation. Let external sounds take you to a deeper level of love, peace, and acceptance. Breathing deeply, call your highest-vibration spirit guides to come and gather around you. With each breath, let everything that stands between you and your guides fade away. Like sediment settling in a glass of water, the veils between the two worlds become clearer, cleaner, and more transparent. You might experience a physical sensation of energies lifting away as you become lighter and lighter. You do not need to know the nature of what is lifting away. As you stay relaxed, with your mind focused and clear, continue to let go, and let go, releasing veil after veil.

As you become clearer and more peaceful, your perception of the subtle energies around you becomes more acute. You begin to sense and feel the presence of your spirit helpers all around you. Start sending your love to your spirit guides. Mentally ask your spirit guides to draw closer so you can meet them. If you'd like, quietly affirm: "I am open and ready to perceive and meet my highest-vibration spirit guides."

Notice the presence of your guides as you receive stronger, clearer impressions. Ask your spirit guide to send you love and to surround you with his or her love. Gently observe what is happening, staying calm and peaceful, maintaining an attitude of loving acceptance.

Introduce yourself and wait for a reply. Ask what role this guide is going to play in your life. Ask how he or she will help you develop your mediumship. Ask if there is something your spirit guide would like to say to you. Wait for a reply. Ask how you can call upon your spirit guide and receive the answer. When you feel that your meeting with your spirit guide is complete, gently return your awareness to your physical surroundings.

Practices to Deepen Your Connection with Your Spirit Guides

The best way to establish a deeper, more purposeful connection with your spirit guides is to regularly enlist their help in your daily life. The practices below will help you experience frequent contact with your guides. Over a period of months you will come to realize that you have gotten into the habit of receiving regular high-quality insight and guidance for yourself.

Practice: Get in the Habit of Asking for Help

One of the laws of the universe is that we have to ask for help, because no one—not even our spirit loved ones or spirit helpers—has the right to interfere with the exercise of our free will. Our spirit helpers do what they can to be of assistance to us without crossing the boundaries of free will. However, I think they can help us even more when we specifically request their assistance.

I often ask for help finding a parking space in the famously congested downtown of Washington, DC, or in front of the entrance to my apartment building, especially when I come from a long trip with luggage to haul. I ask for help in taking the smoothest routes when I'm traveling, as well as with the purchase of airline tickets. I ask for assistance with writing, with teaching my workshops and circles, and with finding lost or misplaced items. When my kids are getting ready to take exams and they request it, I usually ask for spirit help on their behalf. I ask when I try to understand something, whether it is how to assemble a piece of furniture or an event that happened in my life years back. I find that since I've started asking my guides for help, a lot of things run much smoother and I don't get nearly as frustrated as I used to.

Practice: Ask Your Spirit Guides for a Gift

This exercise is a wonderful opportunity to engage your spirit guides on a daily basis. It is also a great tool to help you deepen your understanding of how your guides use symbols in their communication with you. But most of all, it gives your guides the opportunity to convey higher spiritual philosophy to you.

At the end of your morning meditation, ask your spirit guides to bring you a gift that has relevance for the day ahead. By keeping your request broad, your guides will have room to work with you—and to surprise you in the process!

Please resist the temptation of asking for predictive gifts, such as "How is my day going to be?" or "Am I going to get that job offer today?" or "Is Andy going to call me today?" Requests for predictions are much too limited. Oftentimes they are simply based on ego or petty concerns that your spirit guides couldn't care less about.

After you ask for the gift, wait a few minutes. If nothing happens, then continue to focus and restate your request. If still nothing happens, then imagine the gift. (That's what I did the first time I did this exercise.) You may imagine a package wrapped in amethyst-colored paper, with a soft, silk bow of red and gold. Though initially you may feel as if you are making it up, very quickly you will come to recognize the hand of Spirit. The gift might come to you in your thoughts, especially when an image or an idea suddenly comes to you.

Pay close attention to every aspect of the gift. How is it presented? Is the gift wrapped? How is it wrapped? You will find that every tiny part of it has significance.

Whatever the gift is, accept the first one that comes, even if you have no clue what it could possibly mean. Accept the gift and thank your spirit guides. Be sure to note the details of your gift in your journal.

Before you go to sleep, think about your gift and examine your day to find the meaning of the gift. If you cannot see a connection between the gift and how your day went, ask your guides to help you understand the gift's significance.

Practice: Ask Your Guides for a Message from Your Environment

As you are out and about during your day, ask questions of your spirit guides and watch for the answers. Ask only one question at a time. Don't ask: "Should I quit my job, move to Hawaii, and start a restaurant?" That's three questions. Instead ask, "How can I tell that the time has come to quit my job?" or "Is it a good idea to move to Hawaii?"

The answer might appear in the phrase of a song that you hear on the radio. One of my clients had been divorced and had managed to stay on cordial terms with her ex-husband. One day she was wondering whether there was anything to his newfound attentiveness toward her. Just at that moment, a song came on the radio: Whitney Houston's "I Will Always Love You." My client realized that she, too, still loved her ex-husband. She took the message to heart, and they reunited.

Your answer might show up on someone's vanity plate. I often receive messages from other people's license plates. Several years ago, I really wanted to go to Shenandoah National Park, but kept putting it off in favor of what I considered more urgent priorities. During the course of an errand, I was driving on the Capital Beltway when a car merged in front of me. The license plate read "Shen&oa." With that, I realized my desire to go to Shenandoah wasn't just a whim; it was indeed something I needed to do. I took the next exit, went back home to grab my hiking boots and a bag lunch, and headed out to Shenandoah National Park. While there, I received the inspiration for an outdoor workshop that I have been teaching twice a year since then.

Another example occurred several years ago while I was stuck in the left-turn lane. I was wondering whether a friend I lost contact with would ever contact me again. In that moment a car drove past me on my right. The license plate read "He Will." Sure enough, the friend contacted me two months later.

Yet another time I was driving and wondering whether someone told me the truth about something that was important to me. In that moment, a car passed me. Its license plate recommended "Trust."

If you ask a question and you don't notice anything special within the next few minutes, it could be that it's not yet time to have the question answered, or perhaps you worded the question ambiguously. In my experience, straightforward questions tend to receive straightforward answers.

Practice: Ask Your Guides for a Message from a Book

On occasion, ask your spirit guides to give you insight into a situation or problem by directing you to a passage in a book. The process is very simple, and can be done at home, at a bookstore, or at the library.

State the problem that you need help with, and let yourself be guided to a book on a shelf. Just go by your gut feeling. Don't worry about the subject of the book that draws your attention. Whatever book you pull out, trust that it is the right one.

Pick up the book and let it open to whatever page it wants to open to. Let your eyes be drawn to a certain passage on the page. The print might stand out to you, or perhaps you will see a special light on the section that applies to you. Read the section and think about how it applies to your question. Now, act on the guidance you receive.

You will find that you will receive very direct and to-the-point instruction, insight, or guidance in this way. By acting on the help given, you let your guides know that you value their input. This encourages them to bring you more of it.

For example, when I was struggling with writing the natural law section of this book, I finally asked my guides to direct me to a passage in a book that would help me eliminate the difficulties. As soon as I made my request, I was drawn to the bookshelf in my bedroom. When I reached out, my hand was drawn to Edgar Cayce's *A Search for God, Book II*.[5] When I opened the book at random, my eyes were drawn to the following passage:

> We should present ourselves as channels of blessings for others. To be a blessing may demand

5   Edgar Cayce, *A Search for God, Book II* (A.R.E. Press, 1996), 63.

that we present ourselves as a living sacrifice, as a living example to others.

I immediately understood that I needed to introduce natural law within a framework that allows for a medium's best and highest functioning. I also understood that I needed to make the chapter more engaging by adding practices drawn from my own experience.

Questions & Answers

I didn't meet a spirit guide.

In my workshops, people usually succeed in making contact with their guides, but on rare occasions I have had students who don't—at least, not on the first attempt. If you did not make contact the first time, give it time and repeat the process on subsequent days. If, in spite of your good-faith attempts, you are still not making contact, please reread chapter 1, "How Mediumship Works," to help you identify the particular block you are dealing with. Repeat the "Thinning the Veils of Separation" process on subsequent days and at regular intervals. Just like you didn't learn to drive a car in just one afternoon, you can't become a full-fledged medium in one sitting. Continue to practice.

I'm not receiving my guides' names.

This is quite common. There are several reasons for this. First, names are just not as important in the spirit world, and second, some of our guides come from cultures where names were held sacred and were not shared casually. It's important to remember that relationships with our spirit guides develop over time, just as relationships do in the physical. If you don't receive a name, do not despair. Just know that as you do your best to live a spiritual life, your guides will reveal more about themselves. And when they do, you know that a high honor has been bestowed upon you.

I haven't been able to contact a guide whom I met several weeks ago.
Don't worry about it. Guides make their presence known when they want to. Usually they operate quietly in the background without our being aware of their presence. Sometimes entire months go by when I am not particularly aware of the presence of particular guides, so what you are experiencing is quite normal.

Is it possible that I don't have any spirit guides?
No. Everyone has spirit guides, but not everyone is aware of them or knows a lot about them. There are plenty of competent mediums who don't know who their spirit guides are—and that's fine. You might never learn this information, so please don't get hung up on knowing your guides.

How do I know which spirit guide to call upon?
Spirit guides are multitalented and multidimensional. With time you will learn the strengths of each your guides. Instead of worrying about whether to call upon a gatekeeper, master teacher, or spirit companion, I would suggest calling upon all of your guides when help is needed, and let them sort it out among themselves. I usually go to my favorite spirit guide first. If a situation falls completely out of his realm of expertise, then he will bring in others who are better suited to answer a particular question.

*My spirit guide doesn't seem to come around
anymore, but I am aware of new guides.*

Your initial spirit guide could have been a transitional guide. When someone first begins spiritual development, his or her vibration might not yet be high enough to allow for the perception of spirit guides. In that case, a transitional guide might help in the spiritual progression, until the medium is ready to work with a higher-vibration guide. Please note that difference in vibration does not denote difference in quality.

Do our spirit guides hang around constantly?

No, they don't, actually. Our guides live full lives in the spirit world. They are not hovering over us like helicopter parents. Often our guides are otherwise occupied; at other times they leave us alone as we go about our lives. This does not mean, however, they have abandoned us. I sometimes go through weeks when I am not aware of any special interaction with my guides. However, if I really needed them or if my life were threatened, they would be instantly with me.

8

Is It Spirit Communication or Imagination?

Because mediums receive spirit impressions through the spiritual senses, beginners often find it difficult to recognize spirit communication. Beginners want to know how to tell the difference between spirit communications and their own thoughts, feelings, imagination, daydreams, self-talk, and so forth. The gift of discernment develops with time as you grow in your meditation practice and self-knowledge, and as you practice self-observation.

How to Distinguish Spirit Communication from Your Thoughts

Luckily, it is rather easy to recognize a thought; its main characteristic is that its antecedent can be traced back to the thought's origin in everyday life. That is, you can backtrack: "I was cleaning the car when I thought about my upcoming trip to the grocery store, which caused me to remember that I had forgotten my wallet." Information from Spirit, on the other hand, tends to be completely unrelated to whatever we had just been thinking about. As one medium puts it, "When I suddenly find myself thinking about people, situations, or things that are completely unrelated to myself and my life, then I know that I am receiving Spirit communication."

Spirit information has a fresh feel to it and typically runs counter to our habitual inclinations or preferences. For example, I was separated for two and a half years before I finally filed for divorce. Throughout this time, I kept having the recurring thought, "Go ahead and file for divorce. Don't waste time. You need to take care of this now." I wasn't ready, though, so I dragged my feet and procrastinated. When I finally filed for divorce, an important matter went against me, in part because I had delayed for so long. My spirit people had done what they could to urge me to take action, so in the end I only had myself to blame.

Another characteristic of thoughts is that they come and go and tend to change over time. On the other hand, Spirit messages are consistent and repetitive. Spirit won't suggest today that you file for divorce and backtrack tomorrow. A fellow medium puts it this way: "When I push a thought away, but it keeps coming back, I know it's coming from Spirit, and I need to pay attention."

Spirit will repeat the message in many different creative ways. You might not only hear the idea repeatedly in your mind, but also when you turn on the radio and suddenly a song tells you to go ahead and do what Spirit has suggested. When I was in denial of the need of filing for divorce, each time I turned on the car radio, I'd hear the Fleetwood Mac song "Go Your Own Way."

How to Distinguish
Clairvoyance from Your Imagination

Observe how your clairvoyant images differ from your daydreams and regular imagination. For example, my clairvoyant images arrive with a very sharp and distinct energy. The image comes quickly, in very bright colors, and seems to gather toward an energetic center. Also, my clairvoyant scenes appear against a black background. Obviously, that is very different from my ordinary, everyday imagination. The images of my imagination arise more slowly, but are larger than life. They have a softer, fuzzier focus than my clairvoyant images, but they present in full view, as in the movies.

How to Distinguish Clairaudience from Self-Talk

During the next couple of days, become more self-observant; notice how you talk to yourself and what subjects your self-talk focuses on. In my experience, self-talk tends to be focused on the mundane. I have noticed that when I talk or think to myself, my thoughts are always in the first-person singular. "I should do this and that today." "I have to remember to call so-and-so." "I've got an appointment with the dentist at 3:30 p.m." When I hear the voice of Spirit through my clairaudience, I'm addressed in the second-person singular, and there is fresh tone to the message. I hear things like, "Why don't you try this?" or "Wouldn't it be nice if you did that?"

Most people have a rather vocal, disapproving inner critic. The tone of the inner critic is usually judgmental and negative. The inner critic might say things like, "Who are you to write a book?" "What do you know about writing? Nothing!" or "You are too fat, too old, too inexperienced, not creative enough, not witty enough, yak, yak, yak!"

Spirit's voice, on the other hand, is usually upbeat and positive. Spirit might say things like, "You won't feel so sluggish in the morning if you eat fruit before bedtime instead of ice cream." Or, "Go ahead and write your book. We'll help you find the information you'll need." Or, "If you write a little every day, you'll have a book by the end of the year."

Also, pay attention to where you hear your thoughts. I have noticed that I hear clairaudiently in my left ear, so when I hear a voice on my left side, I know it's my clairaudience and I better pay attention. If the voice is just in the center of my head, I know it is self-talk.

How to Distinguish Clairsentience from Your Feelings

The best way to learn to distinguish your own feelings from clairsentience is through regularly monitoring your emotions and physical sensations. Several times a day, stop what you are doing and check in with your feelings. What are you feeling? How does your body feel? Are you tired, cranky, sad, vulnerable, happy, exuberant, and confident? Does your body feel relaxed and healthy? What aches and pains are typical for you?

When a person comes into your room, home, or cubicle at work, check your feelings again. How have they changed from the base feeling you've had throughout the day? Then, check back with your base feeling. If it is unchanged, but you are noticing feelings of sadness, depression, or perhaps achy knees, you might be picking up on someone else's feelings.

If you are having a fine day and suddenly you notice that you are feeling unsettled, think back. When did the unsettled feeling begin? What triggered it? Did something upsetting or annoying happen that flipped your trigger? Whom did you talk to or interact with? When we trace the feeling back to its origin, we often discover that what we are feeling has nothing to do with us.

If you are very sensitive and you are easily affected by the moods of others, stop and ask yourself, "Whose feeling is this?" I always get a clear answer when I ask myself this question. If it's not my own feeling, then I just let it go.

You can release the conditions and emotions of others through visualization. You can intend and imagine that earth's natural magnetism is drawing all unwanted energy off of you, transmuting it into beauty and light. You can also splash cold water on your face or drink a glass of water to break an energetic connection, whether it is with a person in the physical realm or with a spirit person (see chapter 14, "Nurturing Your Mediumship Over the Long Haul").

How to Recognize Your Intellectual Censor

Sometimes we don't want to share information that we receive for another person because it reminds us so much of our own life that we don't trust what we received. I call this the intellectual censor. This is an example of how it works: You are exchanging readings with another development-circle participant. You are relaxed, and spirit impressions come to you. In your mind's eye you see your exercise partner driving in a red car on the freeway and suddenly getting hit by another car. Instead of accepting this image and describing it to your partner, you talk yourself out of it. "I'm making this up because on the way to the class I almost got hit by a red car!" Later on, you hear your exercise partner telling another circle participant about how a red car on the freeway hit her just a few days ago and how she's now waiting for the insurance money.

Or perhaps you tripped on a rock during a recent hike and hurt your hip. Now you are sitting in a reading, and you experience hip pain. Is it your own hip that's acting up, or is it that of a spirit communicator? My agreement with the Great Mystery and with my spirit helpers is that everything that I feel, hear, sense, smell, taste, or experience after the opening prayer is valid spirit communication, even if I happen to have the same physical conditions that the spirit communicator had.

So, if every person that comes through in reading after reading is a balding, big-bellied guy named George, then say it anyway. Just because you've brought three of them through in previous sittings does not preclude your current sitter from having a big-bellied

George in her family tree. Relay the information that you receive. And remember, your spirit guides have a sense of humor. They might also just be putting you through an exercise in trust.

Exercise: How to Distinguish True and False Information

Get together with a friend or establish a phone date with a friend. Ask him or her to read you a list of statements you prepared about yourself, your life, your likes, dislikes, or other aspects of yourself. Make sure that some of the statements are true, some are false, and some are ambiguous. Ask your friend to pause for a while between statements. During that pause, observe the differences among how true, false, and ambiguous statements feel to you.

For me, true statements generate the feeling of clarity, like clear, cool water running through my body. One of my students feels a tap on the shoulder when she correctly understands spirit information. Others experience a sense of expansion when they are receiving true information.

Many people experience false information as a tightening in the body, a contraction in the stomach, or a contraction in the throat. To me, false information feels flat and empty. Sometimes I experience false information as lips moving but there is no feeling behind it. One of my friends gets a sick feeling when hearing incorrect information. Another sees a traffic light turning green when he is given correct information and turning red with false information.

Ambiguous information for me has a vague, wishy-washy feel to it, like a set of scales that has a hard time coming into balance. Some people don't get any feeling at all with ambiguous statements.

9

Ping-Pong with Spirit: The Process of Spirit Communication

In my development circle, I have noticed that people often have difficulty understanding how mediums receive information from the spirit world. Most beginning mediums assume that their spirit communicators will bring a constant stream of information in the way a television set or radio streams information to the passive observer or listener.

On rare occasions when you have a particularly great connection, or a very animated, outgoing spirit communicator, this might indeed be true. Usually, though, the process of receiving spirit information is much more arduous and requires great focus and concentration on the part of the medium.

Indeed, communicating with a spirit person is very much like having a conversation with a person in the physical realm. Both parties take turns speaking, listening, and trying to understand each other. The only difference is that in mediumship, the conversation occurs through the mind of the medium. In other words, we send our thoughts to the spirit people, and they send their responses back to us.

This back-and-forth process is very much like playing a game of ping-pong. However, the point of a game of Spirit Ping-Pong is to make sure that you hit the ball so that your partner can return it to you. In Spirit Ping-Pong you play for win-win. Each party scores a point as the partner receives the ball and then hits it back across the line where the other party can likewise receive it.

Each piece of information that a spirit person relays is a precious. Your spirit communicators would not want you to miss important details. That is why they give only one piece of information at a time. When you've received a piece of information, acknowledge it. If you don't understand something, ask for clarification!

Step 9: Begin a Mental Dialogue with the Spirit People

Before you try this, please make sure you read through the entire instructions. Under each part of the steps, I provide an example in parenthesis to illustrate how the mental dialogue works.

Once you have familiarized yourself with this step, go into your sacred space, open with prayer, and follow steps 1 through 8 of the connecting process. What happens next includes:

1. A spirit person hits the first ball toward you when he or she provides the first piece of evidence. If you find that no spirit person is reaching out to you, you can initiate the conversation by asking: "Who is here with me?" The first bit of information could be a feeling, a physical sensation, or a thought. If you are clairaudient, you might hear spoken words or songs. If you are clairvoyant, you might see a symbol or an image in your mind's eye or in your "imagination." (For example, you might suddenly think of a nice big pepperoni pizza.)

2. In order for the game to go somewhere, you now have to hit the ball back to your guide and spirit communicator. As medium, you hit the ball back by acknowledging the first bit of information. (You think: "Okay. Pizza!")

3. If you receive no further information, your spirit communicator might have missed the ball, so you pick up another one and hit it across the veil by asking for additional information. (Continuing with the example above, you might ask: "Okay, who likes pizza?" Or: "Who is talking about pizza?")

4. Your spirit communicator then hits the ball back by providing the next piece of information. (For example, you might feel a sharp pain in your right leg, accompanied by the sensation of having pins stuck in your shoulder.)

5. You then hit the ball back to your spirit communicator by acknowledging these sensations. ("Okay. Sharp pain in the right leg. Got it. Now, what happened to your shoulder?")

6. The spirit person will then answer your question. (Continuing with our example, you then receive the impression of an elderly man in his eighties. You have a sense of a sudden fall, and you get the distinct idea that this is what caused the shoulder injury and that he needed surgery to repair the damage.)

7. You hit the ball back by summarizing the information you have received so far. ("Pizza, pain in the right leg, elderly man in his eighties fell and broke his shoulder, and he needed surgery to repair the damage.")

Now, this might seem like a cumbersome process, but with time, as you work with your spirit helpers, they will come to understand how much information you can handle at a time. Eventually it gets to the point where the information comes in more fluently without you having to ask so many questions.

Practice: Give Your Spirit Guides Feedback

It is a good practice to periodically review your meditations, practices, spirit communications, and psychic experiences with your spirit guides. You will find that with occasional feedback to your spirit guides, your ability to receive information from the spirit world will increase.

For example, you can tell them how you have been receiving information from the spirit world, what came in clearly, and what was unclear. Let them know if information comes in too fast and ask them to go a little slower next time. Or ask if they would please speed things up a little if it comes in too slowly. If there is evidence that you consistently miss or bungle, tell your guides to work with you so that you will be accurate.

10

Symbols and Your Filing System

As you develop your mediumship, you will find that the spirit people love to use symbolism in their communications with you. A symbol is a visual image that represents an idea, concept, action, or feeling. You can think of symbols as spirit shorthand to quickly and efficiently convey an idea or concept. The spirit people will always use the shortest and most efficient way to deliver as much information as possible.

Some symbols are straightforward and almost universally unambiguous. For example, a red octagon means "stop" almost anywhere. A skull and crossbones warns of lethal poisons. A green traffic light means go. A heart shape means love. A diamond ring refers to commitment, engagement, and marriage. A cake with burning candles on top represents a birthday.

Often, though, the interpretation of symbols is highly subjective, as it is based upon a person's experience and frame of reference. For example, let's assume that a spirit communicator shows the image of a snake. Your interpretation of a snake depends largely on how you feel about snakes. If you come from a strong Judeo-Christian background, you might associate snakes with the fall of Adam and Eve in the Garden of Eden. In that case, you might interpret snake to signify temptation or betrayal. Or, if a snake once bit you, the symbol might warn you of impending danger and pain. Someone with a medical background might think of the snakes in the caduceus and associate the image with healing. To a herpetologist—or a snake charmer—snakes might simply signify work. In my life, snakes have always appeared just before major life changes, so that's what they mean to me.

Everything in the physical realm can also serve as a symbol, including plants, features of the natural environment, animals, planets, as well as man-made objects, including architecture. A red maple leaf might represent the nation of Canada. Bears imply great strength as well as a need for periods of hibernation. Cats might symbolize independence, and dogs could symbolize loyalty. Mountains might represent challenges or the quest for spiritual knowledge. We might associate the planet Jupiter with good fortune. The Taj Mahal could be a symbol of mourning the loss of a great love. The World Trade Center's Twin Towers might symbolize terrorism or heroic acts in spite of overwhelming odds.

Symbols can have both literal and symbolic meanings. The image of a car driving on a highway can symbolize how a person is moving though life. Yet it could also refer to the sitter's car and indicate that there is something that needs to be fixed or a car that was significant to the spirit person conveying the message. Sometimes several possible interpretations apply. Your dad might have been killed in a car accident, and he might be showing up in a reading to remind you to replace your brakes.

There are a number of symbolism- and dream-interpretation dictionaries on the market to help you when you have absolutely no clue as to what a symbol could mean. In general, though, I recommend you develop your own associations. The best way to build your own interpretations is to ask yourself what a given symbol means to you. Once you have established a set of meanings, use them consistently. This will help your mediumship become more precise and accurate.

Exercise: Discover the Meaning of Symbols through Journaling

Let a symbol pop into your mind. Set a timer for five minutes, and start journaling about the symbol. Write as fast as you can. Don't stop and don't edit; just focus on writing about the symbol. If you can't think of a symbol, here are some you can journal about:

- Bungee cord
- Silver
- Lollipop
- Foil

- Bridge
- Overpass
- Train
- Hammer
- Daisy
- Frame
- Rock
- Sequoia
- Avalanche
- Saltwater taffy
- Nail
- Desert
- Ferris wheel

Exercise: Choose a Symbol to Represent Various Situations in Your Life

- Your relationship with your mother
- Your relationship with your father
- Your relationship with your boss
- Your bank account
- Your career
- Your attitude toward life
- Your attitude toward your ex
- The state of your health

+ Your marriage or love relationship
+ Your diet
+ Your home environment
+ Your neighborhood
+ Your career goals
+ Your guilty secret

Quickly write down the first symbol that comes to mind as you think about each situation. After you have chosen your symbols, spend five minutes journaling about how each symbol applies to its situation. This additional exploration is likely to yield more information that can help you make positive changes. For example, if your bank account looks like a leaky faucet, you might decide to look through your account statement and identify expenses you can reduce or eliminate altogether.

Exercise: Symbol Assessment Reading

Think about an area of your life about which you'd like to receive insight, and ask your spirit guides to show you the situation—as it is now—in symbolic form. Pay close attention to what you are shown and observe each detail carefully. Spirit never wastes energy, so everything that you perceive is part of the message. For example, if you are asking for a symbol to represent the condition of a relationship, you might be shown a tree. Pay attention to the species as well as the season it is in. Note whether its bark and roots look healthy. Does it grow in rich soil or on craggy rock that its roots can barely anchor the tree in?

Exercise: Take a Symbol Divination Walk

Think about a situation in your life that you would like to understand better. Keep the question simple, and make sure you only ask one thing.

Avoid "should" questions, because your spirit helpers will never tell you what you should do. Avoid double-barreled questions, such as, "What do I need to know about moving to Los Angeles and working in the movie industry?" You've just asked two questions, and each one is open-ended. The same is true for "either/or" questions. Each should be explored separately.

Once you have selected your question, go outside and take a short walk. Your walk should contain changes of direction, such as walking an entire city block, skirting the circumference of your garden, or hiking a full circuit in nature. As you begin to walk, without thinking, quickly notice the first two things that catch your eye and write them down. Walk to the next corner or bend in the path, and turn in a new direction. Once again, jot down the first two things that catch your eye. Keep walking until it's time to make the next turn. After you've made your turn, once again notice the first two things that stand out for you and jot them down. Explore in your journal how the things that you noticed answer your question.

If you doubt the validity of this exercise to give you good insight in symbolic form, then take the same walk at a later time and notice all the things that you overlooked on the first trip.

Mediumship and Your Mental Filing System

Your spirit guides are able to access your mental filing system and your associations with various symbols and life situations. My father, for example, was a businessman who always wore a suit. So when spirit people want to let me know that they were businessmen, they show themselves wearing suits. I grew up in Europe at a time when people still wore black to indicate they were mourning the death of a significant loved one. So when a spirit person appears wearing black, I know that he or she was either widowed or at some time had buried a child.

Your spirit helpers are also intimately familiar with your general knowledge base, which of course extends well beyond your knowledge of symbolism. If you love music and know many songs by heart, the spirit people will often make you aware of special songs they shared with loved ones or that have special symbolic meaning to the sitter. Mediums who are film buffs often receive information from the spirit world containing pertinent references to movies.

Anything you do to extend your general knowledge base also expands your mediumship. If you decide you want to familiarize yourself with various dog breeds, your spirit helpers will be aware of this, and in the future you will be able to see spirit dogs more precisely—instead of as small, medium-size, or large furry blurs with wagging tails. If you are pregnant and studying baby-name books for inspiration, you might discover an added bonus of suddenly being able to perceive a broader range of spirit names. If you develop an interest in theater and start reading and attending plays, you may start to bring through spirit communicators who shared the same interest and who loved the same plays you do.

In other words, what you do in your everyday physical life has repercussions in your mediumship. As above, so below, and vice versa. Developing our mediumship is not just about meditation and sitting in development circles. Anything that enriches your life and your mind in the physical realm also helps expand your mediumship. Indeed, you might want to get into the habit of scheduling monthly forays into unfamiliar areas to enrich your life and your base of experiences.

11

Evidence and Spirit Messages

When mediums connect with the spirit people in a public demonstration, a private sitting, or a circle, they need to establish a body of precise and unique information called "evidence" so the sitter can recognize the spirit communicator. Establishing a body of evidence is a little like detective work. You have to be observant of what the spirit people share with you and be able to pass this information on to the sitter. You also need to establish a mental dialogue with your spirit communicator so as to ask him or her for pertinent details.

It is best to have a list of required evidence in your mind that you ask for every time so your spirit guides know what you expect. This helps them brief potential spirit communicators in advance of your reading or mediumship demonstration. It also helps them to screen out spirit people who might not be willing to bring solid evidence. This process provides your work with structure and helps you quickly establish the identity of the sitter's spirit loved one. A basic structure of required evidence is outlined below.

The initial tier is composed of basic information that establishes the "skeleton outline" of the spirit person; this information is the foundation that makes it clear to the sitter who is communicating. As a beginning medium, I would not expect you to be able to perceive all of the information listed below. However, as you become more proficient and adept at receiving information from the spirit world, you should strive to include at least four or five items from each tier of evidence for every spirit person you connect with:

- Relationship to the sitter
- Age at death
- Cause of death
- Circumstances surrounding his or her passing
- Physical characteristics
- Name
- Occupation
- Address

After you have established the first tier of information, the second tier establishes the spirit communicator as the distinctive, unique, quirky, and colorful individual that he or she was during physical life. It is the kind of amazing evidence that you could not possibly know unless you are indeed in contact with the sitter's spirit loved one. The more details you can describe, the more comfort and healing the sitter will feel. The second tier includes the following items:

+ Personality

+ Character

+ Hobbies, interests, and habits

+ Foods they liked to eat

+ Special possessions

+ Characteristics that made the spirit communicator unique

+ Special memories and stories

+ Shared memories with the sitter

+ Family and friends in spirit who are with them on the other side

+ Pets in the spirit world

Although it might seem obvious why these pieces of evidence are useful as the foundation of the spirit conversation, let me expand on some of the subtleties to watch for when in dialogue with a spirit person. Also, for the clearest transmission of information, it is best not to ask the sitter for detail in the way of response or confirmation as the information is presented. All the medium needs to know is whether the information is understood or if more questioning of the spirit visitor on a certain topic is needed; otherwise, the medium's mind might become distracted with the sitter's explanations and the reading loses its authenticity.

Relationship to the Sitter

This is a key piece of evidence and refers to mother, father, husband, wife, brother, sister, son, daughter, grandmother, grandfather, uncle, aunt, cousin, in-law, friend, neighbor, godmother, godfather, colleague, etc.

It is important that you correctly identify the relationship of the spirit communicator to the sitter. If you misidentify the relationship, the subsequent evidence that is connected with your spirit communicator won't fit the sitter's relative. Sitters are often very literal-minded, so if you say "father" when it's instead their Uncle Bob who is coming through, they will probably just shake their heads, because they won't even be thinking about Uncle Bob. Few sitters have the presence of mind to recognize your mistake at the time of the reading.

Unless you are clairaudient and the spirit people tell you how they are related, the relationship can be difficult to determine. One of my students knows how people are related when she sees an image of her own family members. If she sees her grandmother, she knows the spirit communicator is the sitter's grandmother. If she sees her sister, she knows she's talking to the sitter's sister. Another student has done a lot of research on family genealogy. When he gives mediumship demonstrations, the spirit people show him their positions on the family tree.

If you are clairsentient, you have to see how the relationship feels to you: Does the spirit communicator feel like a father? Or does he feel like a brother? Does he feel like an uncle? If you are clairsentient, you might experience extra challenges in trying to figure out how the spirit people are connected with your sitter. But don't give up. Focus on the feelings between the spirit person and the sitter. Do you sense there was love between them? Does it feel like the love between family members or like romantic love?

Occasionally when you are out and about or at a gathering, tune in to the people around you. See if you can determine their relationship to one another. Feel the energy between fathers and sons, mothers and daughters, and whatever relationships present themselves. In actual readings, nailing this aspect might take a while, but if you are determined to establish the relationship to the sitter every time, eventually you will reach your goal.

Age at Death

Unless the spirit people are very specific and you are absolutely sure you are correct, it can be better to give an age range than a specific number. If you say Grandpa died at age eighty-four when in fact he was eighty-six, your sitter might say that you are wrong. If you say that he appears to have passed in his mid-eighties, the sitter will say you are correct.

Be aware that the spirit people can show themselves as they looked when they were young and in good health. Therefore, you cannot conclude that they died young based on their appearance. It is best to just ask, "How old were you when you died?"

Cause of Death

Of course, the cause of death can include a myriad of examples. Some common ones I have encountered are cancer, smoking-related illnesses, pneumonia, appendicitis, heart attack, stroke, accidents, suicide, and murder. Keep in mind that symptoms that are presented to you might feel similar among illnesses or events involving certain parts of the body.

If you are clairaudient, the spirit people might tell you what they died from. If you are clairvoyant, you might be able to see exactly what happened. If you are clairsentient, you might feel the cause of death in your body. For example, with cancer, you might sense a painful wasting away, or you might smell the chemotherapy drugs. A heart attack might feel like a sudden explosion in your chest. If someone died from a shooting, you might have the sensation of a bullet passing through you.

If you don't receive any information about the cause of death, it was probably very sudden. In many of these cases, the spirit people don't remember what happened, because they were gone instantly. Occasionally, you will connect with spirit people who took their own lives. Suicides are often reticent about the cause of their deaths.

Circumstances Surrounding His or Her Passing

This refers to events that took place around the time a person died, and might be very important to the sitter. This can include events in the weeks or hours before death. This information can include events that precipitated the death, medical procedures, their last conscious memories, and events that took place when the dying person was in a coma, such as last rites.

Physical Characteristics

This refers to the spirit communicator's appearance, such as height, weight, body build, hairstyle, and overall attractiveness. Pay attention to visible physical ailments suggested by hearing aids, glasses, crutches, a wheelchair, a cane, and the like.

Please note that physical appearance in and of itself is often not enough evidence to convince your sitter that you are really connecting with a deceased loved one. Physical appearance can be very generic, as in the case of a grandmother with gray hair, cut in an older woman's style, or wearing an apron and baking a cake. Most people had grandmothers or great-grandmothers who fit that general description. You might not be able to help giving a generic description, but you should then strive for more information so that this particular grandmother becomes the unique and distinct person that the sitter remembers.

Even if you don't consider yourself clairsentient, you should always pay attention to how your body feels when you connect with a spirit person. Do you feel your body contract or expand as you as try to determine whether the person was tall or short, heavy or slender? Do you suddenly have the sense there was something wrong with the person's vision? Do you feel the pressure of a hearing aid in your ears? Do you have a sense of the body being stooped or a hand holding on to a cane? Or do you perhaps feel a leaden heaviness suggesting that the person suffered from paralysis?

Names

It is wonderful if the spirit people give you their names, but it is important to realize that names in and of themselves are not evidential. Even if your sitter were in tears when you correctly came up with the name "Roger," you would still need to bring forth other identifying information. It is not enough to say, "Mary is here," or even, "Mary, Helen, and Abby are here." A name is just a start, and that's all it is.

Also, keep in mind that names are not necessarily the names of the spirit communicator. A name can be a first name, middle name, last name, or the name of a street, location, or building. Oftentimes spirit communicators provide a connecting name, such as the name of other people who were significant to them. It is also possible that a spirit person is concerned about a person on earth by that name. Also, please be aware that you might not hear names, but you could suddenly find yourself thinking of your Aunt Mary or your friend Jimmy when a spirit person wants to convey the name Mary or Jimmy.

If you are clairaudient, please realize you might hear a name incorrectly. For example, you might hear "Ellen" instead of "Helen," "Shawn" instead of "Shonda," "Dolly" instead of "Doris," "Ann" instead of "Andrew," and "Monica" instead of "Veronica." If your sitter doesn't recognize the name, you will have to admit that you might not be hearing the name clearly. Ask if the sitter would recognize a name that sounds very similar to one you mentioned.

The best way to increase your ability to receive the spirit people's names is by paying attention to names in the physical world. If you are one of these people who can't be bothered remembering the names of the people you are introduced to, in all likelihood you won't be able to receive names from the spirit world. To change this limitation, set your intention that from now on you are going to remember the names of the people you meet. When you start to place importance on knowing the names of the people in your daily life, then you'll receive more names from the spirit world.

Occupation

Ask the spirit people what they did for a living. Did they wear a uniform at work? If so, what does the uniform say about their occupation? If they didn't wear a uniform, ask them to show you a picture of their work environment. If you are clairvoyant, you might be able to see what they were doing or perhaps perceive a symbol to help you figure it out.

If you are able to smell the scents from the spirit world, you might be able to smell what they did. For example, offices have a unique odor, as do schools, libraries, hospitals, and laboratories. A car repair shop has its own unique blend of smells that is very identifiable. Someone who did a lot of hard physical labor might smell sweaty. From now on, train yourself to pay attention to smell when you meet people and when you enter buildings, offices, and stores. The more locations you can recognize, the more examples the spirit people have to choose from.

Address

This is something many people do not think to ask, but do request the spirit people give you the addresses where they used to live. Some mediums, like the late British medium Estelle Roberts, are very gifted in receiving exact locations. It is rare to receive that kind of detailed information, but still worthwhile to ask for it. Please note that addresses can be given symbolically. If someone lived on Oak Street, for example, you might see an oak tree or an acorn. If someone lived on Castle Drive, you might receive the idea of a medieval castle. Someone who lived in Washington, DC, could show you a US dollar bill.

Admittedly, it is not easy to receive an exact address. If you keep asking for it, though, you will become good at it! At the very least, however, with practice, you should be able to determine whether spirit people lived in a house or apartment, in the city or country, and the general geographic area.

Personality

Personality refers to the outward expression and overall disposition of a person. This includes traits such as introversion, extroversion, optimism, pessimism, sense of humor, kind-heartedness, level of patience, generosity, temperament, ambition, and so forth. It is usually a lot easier to receive information about the person's personality than it is to receive information about character.

Character

Character includes whether the spirit person was reliable, honest, loyal to their spouses, and ethical, among other aspects. A lot of spirit people have no problem owning up to their character flaws.

Hobbies, Interests, and Habits

The spirit people fondly remember their favorite pastimes. This is the time in a reading when the sitter gets really animated. The spirit people love to show whether they were artistic and good with color, paints, quilting, needlework, knitting, crocheting, woodworking, drafting, or making repairs. They also often indicate whether they enjoyed playing cards or games, loved sports, enjoyed hunting or kayaking, or drank alcohol. These kinds of details are often the ones the sitter relates to best, because these activities are often shared, or commonly discussed or recognized in familial settings.

Foods They Liked to Eat

Eating is one of the great pleasures of life, and the spirit people fondly remember favorite foods. Those who were intimately connected to food might have deep and enduring reputations with loved ones regarding this activity. For example, Aunt Nettie might have been famous for her upside-down cake, so it's likely she might mention it. The spirit people often bring me information about the foods they loved to eat or make, so it's always worth asking!

Special Possessions

These can include jewelry or sports equipment, or collections, such as stamps, photos, or paintings. If Dad had a special coin collection that he was proud of, he could bring that collection into the reading as a piece of evidence. The spirit people use objects and special possessions as means of identifying themselves. The big gaudy ring with a tiger's eye in it could have belonged to a sitter's favorite grandmother. Grandmother, who is now in spirit, shows you the ring so there is no doubt you are communicating with her and not with the sitter's other grandmother.

Characteristics that Made the Spirit Communicator Unique

No two people are the same, and you will find that the spirit people become quite lively when you ask about their idiosyncrasies or special qualities. They might show you they've immigrated from another country and they came by sea. They could demonstrate they loved dancing and participated in dance competitions. Or they might indicate they used to host the family Thanksgiving dinner and each year would bring in three six-foot tables to hold the bounty. One spirit person in a reading once appeared standing next to a deceased celebrity. When I mentioned this to my client, she confirmed that her spirit loved one indeed had a close connection to the celebrity. Another spirit person might let you know that she had a beautiful voice and used to sing in her church's choir. Others might indicate they had a wicked sense of humor and they used to play pranks on people.

Special Memories and Stories

Life is full of unique moments, special events, funny stories, and hilarious interactions the sitter would be able to verify, even if he or she was not involved directly. Perhaps Uncle Jack got thrown from a horse and broke all of his ribs. Maybe there's a funny family story about how little Johnny brought the sprinkler into the house when he was supposed to take a nap. And how about Uncle Pete, the priest who was notorious for cheating in card games? This is the sort of information that really makes a reading come to life and lets the sitter know their loved ones are still themselves.

Shared Memories with the Sitter

Shared memories are recollections of special times that both the spirit communicator and the sitter experienced during the spirit person's lifetime. For example, a deceased husband might talk about his first date with his wife; or a deceased daughter might remember the time the family cat got lost for week; or a wife in the spirit world might come through for her husband with memories of the time when both of them were Peace Corps volunteers in Nigeria and got caught in a market riot.

Realize, though, that just as two people in the physical realm sometimes have completely different recollections of events, the spirit person's recollection can vary from the sitter's. People can be so nervous when they come for a reading they cannot think straight. Sometimes people don't remember things until days after the reading. If this happens to you, then just encourage your recipient to remember you said it and reassure them that in all likelihood the memories will come back to them.

If the sitter cannot at all accept the memories the spirit person brings, there might have been a switch in spirit communicators and the memory could belong to a different person. In this case you might have to ask your recipient if the memory could belong to another spirit person.

Family and Friends in Spirit Who Are with Them on the Other Side

Sitters often worry their loved ones are lonely on the spirit side of life, and they are greatly comforted if you can bring evidence they are in the company of loved ones who have also passed on.

Pets in the Spirit World

Our animal companions give us unconditional love and enrich our life immensely. A lot of people love their pets as much as they love their dearest family members and friends. When I give readings, the spirit people often show me the pets they have had during their lifetimes. Often my sitter's deceased pets will come into the reading to let the sitter know they are fine. People receive great comfort knowing their beloved pets are still alive in the spirit world, so get in the habit of asking the spirit people to show you the pets that are with them.

The Importance of the Message

Once you have thoroughly established the identity of the spirit person by giving an abundance of pertinent evidential information, you should ask about their reason for coming into the reading. Some might just want to say hello; others might be masters of ceremony, bringing in the sitter's spirit loved ones. Most of the time, though, the spirit person has a specific message to relay to the sitter. The message is the reason all of the initial evidence is needed so the sitter is confident of who is communicating. However, the message also often provides yet another level of evidence of identity. One could say the message could just be the cherry on top of the identity cake.

The message could involve almost anything, but I have seen several common subject areas, including:

+ Wanting to express something they didn't get to say before death

+ Validation of end-of-life decisions

+ A desire to make amends

+ A new perspective on an old situation

+ Validating of attempts at spirit contact

+ Validation of dream visits

+ Emotional support for the sitter during life crisis or difficulty

+ Guidance on upcoming events in the sitter's life

Wanting to Express Something They Didn't Get to Say to Before Death

A spirit person often wants to express gratitude for assistance received as he or she was dying. Perhaps a loved one sat by his or her bedside for weeks on end. Or maybe the sitter created recordings of the dying person's favorite music and brought it to the hospital. One of my clients read *The Tibetan Book of the Dead* to his mother as she was dying, and he was deeply moved when his mother came to thank him for this important help.

This category of expression might also include important information that simply was not said before death, for one reason or another. Perhaps the spirit person was hesitant to reveal certain information in life, or didn't realize how worried a loved one would be about something. And sometimes the information is simply practical. I know of one sculptor who returned in spirit to tell an art foundry owner the details of how to finish the patina on a new sculpture project that was in process when he suddenly died.

Validation of End-of-Life Decisions

Modern medicine is able to keep the body alive long after the spirit has gone. As a result, families often have to wrestle with a decision to prolong or discontinue life support. It can be very healing for the sitter to hear their deceased loved one approved of discontinuing life support.

Desire to Make Amends

Life on earth is tough, and none of us gets through life without stepping on other people's toes. On occasion, the spirit people come through to apologize to the sitter for actions taken during their lifetimes. Some people were physically and emotionally abusive and want to ask for forgiveness. Other people were emotionally remote and never said, "I love you." The sitter might desperately need to hear these words.

A New Perspective on an Old Situation

New arrivals in the spirit world undergo a life review, where they get to reexperience their interactions with others. During this process, the deceased get to see how their words, actions, and attitudes impacted others. As a result, they are often willing to let go of long-held opinions and attitudes, and they are eager to share their changes of heart with sitters. I've even seen spirit people who regretted having cut a loved one out of their will and in the reading urged the sitters to do what's right and not what the legal papers say.

Validation of Attempts at Spirit Contact

When people die, they often go to great lengths to let their loved ones know they are still alive. For example, after my father died, my parents' wedding photograph suddenly flew out of a book that had been sitting on a shelf. My mother had kept the wedding photos in an album, so she couldn't figure out how the photo could have even gotten into the book in the first place.

After my grandfather died, during a period of three or four weeks every night—around the time he used to get up for a midnight snack—all the lights would come on in my grandmother's home, and that was in the days before people had timers for their lights. Likewise, after a friend's mother died, a blue heron started to show up in her backyard at the time when she and her mother normally would have spoken on the telephone. This went on for many months, and ceased only after my friend had made it through the worst phase of her bereavement.

The spirit people are able to manipulate radios, televisions, and computers so that these devices start up out of the blue to play their favorite songs or shows, or to display favorite digital photographs of them.

Validation of Dream Visits

The spirit people are able to visit their loved ones while they dream. These visits are real. They are not just an organizing activity of the brain. I believe the main reason for the dream visit is that it is the only time when the bereaved person is finally relaxed enough to be able to perceive the presence of the deceased.

One of the hallmarks of a dream visit is that the dreamer becomes aware of the fact the visitor can communicate even though his or her lips are not moving. Another characteristic of a dream visit is that the spirit visitor often makes it a point to show up in the dreams of several family members within just a few days of the initial visit.

After my father died, one night he visited me in a dream. One of the things that stood out in that visit is that my father wore a tank-top style T-shirt. In life my father was always dressed to the nines and preferred to wear business attire, so the fact that he wore such a shirt was remarkable. Several days later, I called my mother and told her about the dream visit, especially remarking upon the fact that Dad wore the T-shirt. My mother fell silent. Then she told me that days earlier, my father had visited one of my brothers in his dream wearing a tank-top style T-shirt. We never knew the meaning of this unusual style of dress, but I assume that he presented this unusual detail that was so uncharacteristic of him to make us realize he was still with us in spirit and that we weren't dreaming.

Emotional Support for the
Sitter During Life Crisis or Difficulty

Occasionally, people will visit a medium during times of emotional difficulty. In such situations, the spirit communicator might offer valuable insight, comfort, or words of encouragement. Our spirit loved ones are able to arrange lucky breaks for us, bring special opportunities to our attention, and arrange circumstances so we meet the right people or information at the right time.

Guidance on Upcoming Events in the Sitter's Life

The spirit people have a more expanded view than ours of what is going on in our lives. They can give us a heads-up on opportunities and challenges coming our way. For example, a client's father came through in a reading to remind him that he needed to play hardball in negotiating the salary for a position my client had just applied for. However, weeks later during the salary negotiation, my client was so awed by the fact that he had actually landed such a coveted position that he forgot to negotiate and instead accepted the proposed salary. Several months later he found out that other employees with similar skills and a similar work history were earning tens of thousands of dollars more than he was! When he contacted me for another appointment, he suddenly remembered that his father had urged him to negotiate.

Expanding Your List of Required Evidence

The list of evidence presented in this chapter is only a starting point. As your ability to connect with the spirits matures, you will discover that you, too, will have a knack for receiving certain types of specialized evidence. For example, I know a medium who has a knack for receiving highly evidential details about conversations that occurred at the deceased person's memorial service. Another medium I know is a painter. She has a knack for seeing the paintings and art objects that a spirit person possessed during his or her lifetime on earth. So, feel free to expand on the list above and never hesitate to ask for the kind of information that seems to come easily to you.

12

Presenting and Working with the Evidence

Although there are no hard and fast rules that satisfy each and every encounter you might have with a sitter, because everyone's life circumstances and reasons for coming to you are unique, I have found that generally a professional, kind, and thoughtful demeanor is most useful. From this standpoint, a reading can always be respectful, even if the sitter does not get the information that he or she came for, or might even be confused by some of the information that is given. Here are a few guidelines regarding how to convey the messages you receive.

Be Dignified in Your Presentation

Even if you are a beginner, you should always present your mediumship in a professional manner. Remember, a lot of people still think that mediums are either frauds or circus acts. To educate the public, you must hold your mediumship to a high standard and present unique, high-quality evidence.

Describe How You Receive Spirit Information

If you receive the information clairvoyantly, preface your report with, "I see …" If the information comes through clairaudience, say, "I hear …" If you receive impressions through clairsentience, say, "I sense …" or, "I feel …" If you smell something, say, "I smell …" or, "I am aware of the scent of …"

When you present the evidence in this way, you validate your process and provide a context for the information. You also train yourself to pay attention to what you receive through all the spiritual senses. In my development circles, I often notice the mediums who present the evidence with a series of "I get" statements often miss out on the subtler spirit impressions, because they are always waiting for the next big thing to "get."

Always Present the Evidence
through a Series of Statements

"I see a young man who appears to be in his mid-thirties. I sense that he died in a car accident. I hear hip-hop music around him. He brings with him the scent of a hot-fudge sundae. I taste Cherry Coke, and I know that he drank it often."

Don't Present Evidence by
Asking a Series of Yes-or-No Questions

Even if you are correct, your sitters may think you are making lucky guesses. They might not believe you are communicating with their spirit loved ones. Some questions might seem to be so specific that they clinch the spirit person's identity. Still, they are much more compelling if phrased as statements. Consider switching the following questions into "I sense" or "He tells me" statements: "Did your father marry five times?" "Was he forty-five when his first child was born?" "Did he drive a school bus?" "Did he like to play poker?" "Did he win the lottery?" "Did his son crash the family car?"

Working with the Evidence

Verify that Your Sitter Understands
the Information You Receive from Spirit

I like to provide my sitter with about five or six pieces of evidence at a time before I ask if he or she understands the information. For example, I might say, "I am aware of a woman who lived into her nineties. She outlived her husband by twenty-five years. She is your grandmother. Her name was Rose or Rosa. She died in her sleep, and she loved quilting. Do you understand? Please answer yes or no." After the sitter has acknowledged the information, I bring in another group of five or six pieces of evidence.

In this way, you can make sure your reading stays on track. Conversely, if you were to give too many pieces of evidence without checking with your recipient, you might run into trouble—the sitter might not remember the beginning of the evidence, or might get turned off if one piece in a string sounds wrong, even if the rest are correct.

Also, verifying information with the sitter makes it easier to spot when there has been a change in spirit communicators. For example, after Grandma has had her say, Granddad might decide to come into the reading and start sending his own information, though he might not come into your field of clairvoyant vision. If you were to continue giving information without verifying with your sitter, you might not realize that the dentures, the bum leg, the penchant to drive above the speed limit, and the tendency to lose keys don't match with Grandma, but with Granddad. If the sitter had the opportunity to say, "No," to the last four pieces of information, I would ask the communicating spirit person to identify himself clearly and not mix the evidence.

Do Not Edit or Omit Seemingly Incongruent Evidence

You might be tempted to edit or omit information you think might not fit with your sitter or that makes you feel uncomfortable. However, when you leave out information, your sitter might not recognize the spirit person who has come into the reading. You have no way of knowing what might be significant!

Years ago, when I was student medium in a development class, my exercise partner was a very stylish woman with manicured hands and perfectly coiffed hair. The spirit relative who came through for her was a slovenly looking, middle-aged man named Ed with a big belly, disheveled hair, and grease stains all over his shirt. I could not figure out how such an unkempt person could be connected to my very chic sitter. So when I described the spirit person to her, I purposefully omitted the disheveled appearance and the grease-stained shirt.

My exercise partner kept wrinkling her nose and shook her head. "Ed?" she asked. "No, I don't know anybody named Ed." I kept beating around the bush, but the information still didn't make sense to her. Finally, exasperated, I blurted out, "Okay, Ed looks like a slob. His hair is a mess, and there are big grease stains all over his shirt!"

"Oh, my God," my exercise partner exclaimed as she reached for the tissue box. "That's my beloved Uncle Ed! He was my favorite uncle! I've missed him so much! Oh, dear Uncle Ed! I'm sorry, I just didn't recognize him from your initial description!"

Do Not Tailor the Evidence When a Recipient Disagrees

Inexperienced and insecure mediums who haven't developed enough trust in their spirit helpers are sometimes guilty of changing the evidence based on feedback from the recipient. It works like this: You give a stream of detailed evidence; for example, "I am in contact with your father; he died in his late seventies of a heart attack. In his younger days he was a roadie for the Rolling Stones." The client shakes her head and says, "No, my father was forty when he died in an accident. He wasn't a roadie, but I think that he once went to a Rolling Stones concert." The medium then changes the evidence: "As I was saying, your father was in his forties when he died and had chest pain as a result of an accident he had on his way back from a Rolling Stones concert."

There are several problems with backtracking and trying to make the evidence fit the feedback you receive. First of all, it is dishonest, and the recipient might conclude that you are a fraud even if your skills are legitimate. Second, subsequent evidence will also not fit the person's father, because the actual spirit communicator is someone different. Third, a few minutes later the sitter might have an epiphany and recall the initial evidence fits her father's brother. At that point you will have gone so far down the wrong path that the initial spirit communicator is long gone. What could have been a wonderfully evidential reading is now completely bungled.

It is always best to just stick with your evidence. Trust and report what you receive. If the client says, "No," then work with the spirit person to clarify the problem, but *do not* change the evidence so it fits the feedback!

Do Not Rush to Interpret Symbolic Information

Symbolic information is often very unique and highly personal to the spirit communicator, the sitter, or both. A medium can easily throw a reading off course by trying to interpret a symbol.

Describe what you perceive as accurately as you can, and ask whether your sitter understands the symbol. If the sitter nods his or her head, just move on to the next piece of evidence. Do not try to understand what the symbol means to the sitter. It is not your business! Besides, by trying to understand, you interject your conscious mind, and you risk losing your connection with your spirit person.

If the sitter does not understand the symbol, ask if there is a reason why the spirit person would show you this symbol. Most of the time, once the sitter starts to think about it, the meaning will become clear. In the rare event that the sitter still does not have a clue, go back to your spirit communicator and say, "[Sitter's name] does not understand the symbol you've shown. Why are you showing me the symbol? Can you give me the information in a different way?"

I would attempt to interpret a symbol only as a last resort. In that case, I would give the sitter a number of possible interpretations and encourage the person to think about the possible meaning in the days after the reading. Often people just need some time to reflect before they understand a symbolic message.

Do Not Draw Conclusions Based on the Evidence

For example, the spirit communicator might have identified himself as a soldier. A few moments later he might give you an image or the feeling of being in a hot and arid location. Based on these two pieces of information, you might jump to the conclusion that he had been stationed in Iraq, when in fact he was remembering his favorite family vacation in Death Valley National Park (no pun intended). Let the sitter draw conclusions based on what you, the medium, are reporting. When in doubt, or if you have a hunch about something, always go back to the spirit communicator and verify that your hunch is correct.

Never Solicit Information from Your Sitter

You'll often see mediums in public demonstrations say things like, "Do you have a mother in the spirit world? Was she young when she died? Did she have a car accident?" Or, "Who died of a heart attack? What killed Grandpa?" Or, "Who is John to you?"

Mediums who ask such questions give the appearance of fishing for information that they can feed back to the sitter. This practice leaves you vulnerable to the charge that you are not in contact with the spirit world at all, but out to dupe the gullible.

If you have to ask questions, ask your spirit helpers and your spirit communicators. Trust they will help give you the correct information and the right answers.

Provide a Plethora of Evidential Information Before You Launch into the Message

Giving someone a message without giving a plethora of evidence as to who is communicating is like sending a spam email. Why should your sitter trust a message from an unknown sender?

Never Embellish the Evidence or the Message

Don't say Mom was a darling and is sending love to your sitter unless you really feel her love in your heart. It is important to remember that not all spirit people were kind and loving while they were in a physical body. Sometimes you'll bring through spirit people who were downright nasty and abusive to their spouses and children. When you say the sitter's abusive father is coming through with hugs, kisses, and compliments, your sitter might think that either you are on drugs or that you are lying. It is not your job to sugarcoat the evidence or the experience.

Never Predict Death

The majority of human beings are terrified of death. You will erase all the benefits of a reading or spirit greeting when you predict a person's death. Also, keep in mind that a prediction of death could turn into a self-fulfilling prophecy. It is absolutely irresponsible, unethical, and a misuse of your spiritual gifts to plant such an idea in someone's mind.

It is possible that on rare occasions a spirit person might articulate concern about a person who is still alive. You might have the sense that this person's time on earth is running out. Should you tell the recipient about what you are sensing?

If you feel absolutely compelled that the sitter needs to know this, ask the spirit communicators why they are conveying this information to you. What action would they like your sitter to take?

It is then up to you to find a tactful way to convey the spirit's concern without making a death prediction or scaring the sitter. For example, if the sitter's mother is living in another state and you feel that her time to return to Spirit is drawing close, you could say: "Spirit recommends you make time to visit your mother. I feel urgency with this, so please don't delay this trip." If the sitter wants to know why, you can say that the spirit doesn't say why, but that's the message you received.

Beware of Working on the Psychic Level

You can tell that a medium is working strictly on the psychic level—receiving information from the energy field of the sitter instead of from a spirit person—when he or she either gives no evidence or only minimal evidence. When the medium works only on the psychic level, she will immediately talk about matters that relate to the life of the recipient, not the deceased.

In this case, she would probably say something like, "Your mother is standing beside you, and she's telling me that next month you are moving to another state. Watch out with that move, because things won't turn out as you think. There is going to be a problem with the house you're going to move into, and your new job is going to be a challenge, too, because someone in the new office isn't a team player."

While this could be a perfectly valid and valuable message for the recipient, there is no proof of the continuity of life in it. Remember, as a medium, you should always strive to convey healing and comfort through bringing evidence of the continuity of life beyond physical death. Your job is to convey the message that the spirit person wishes to convey—not your own psychic reading of the sitter's circumstances.

13
Development Circles and Home Circles

Developmental Circles

Development circles are usually run by experienced mediums who teach mediumship development. The participants in these circles are typically at various levels of development, ranging from beginning mediums to professional mediums.

If you are serious about the unfolding of your spiritual gifts, participation in a development circle with a qualified teacher is a must. The concentrated energies of the circle are ideal for spirit contact. Most people find it much easier to meditate and connect with the spirit people while they are participating in a development circle than during their daily meditation at home.

Also, each participant brings her or his spirit loved ones to the circle; this gives everyone the opportunity to connect with sitters and spirit people about whom they know nothing. It helps you develop trust and self-confidence in your gifts. It is a wonderful opportunity to continue learning under your spirit helpers' wise tutelage.

Teaching mediums have a band of spirit helpers that facilitate the development of the student mediums in the group. When I teach my development circles, my spirit guides keep me informed of what is going on with each of my students. It is as if I am able to be with everyone at once. I am also able to perceive and connect with the spirit people who are trying to communicate with my students. This allows me to see how much information my students are missing, and it gives me the opportunity to coach them in being more perceptive. The spirit people always tell me when my students are able to perceive them and when they are trying to talk themselves out of their spirit perception.

Depending on the teaching medium's preference, the development circle can be semi-closed or open. In a semi-closed circle, the same group of people meets at regular intervals throughout a stretch of time, each acting as both sitter and medium. My own development circle, for example, meets for eight-week intervals. During these eight weeks, no newcomers are accepted. Ideally, I would run each circle for more than eight weeks; however, few people are willing to commit to more than eight weeks at a time.

The benefit of the semi-closed circle is that the energies build during the course of the eight weeks as the group's spirit guides maximize the group energies for everyone's benefit. The semi-closed circle requires a more serious commitment of each participant, but it also provides an ideal environment where trust builds and student mediums become more willing to take risks in sharing what they perceive.

In an open circle, student mediums participate as they wish. They might show up once or twice, or as often as they like. You might think that an open circle provides the flexibility of testing the waters of mediumship. However, the problem with open circles is that the participants change weekly and the group energy may never build sufficiently to significantly help the development of all the sitters.

Another significant drawback of open circles is that they tend to attract people who don't want to make a commitment to their development or to supporting the development of others in the circle. Open circles often attract needy people with a lot of personal problems who want to use the circle for getting cheap psychic help. Due to the Law of Vibration, such disposition creates a less-than-ideal environment for developing mediums.

When someone is only interested in taking from the group rather than adding to it, and when people bring all their problems to the circle, the energy of the entire circle is significantly affected and diminished. This, in turn, makes it much harder for student mediums to connect with the spirit world. I have seen student mediums give up on mediumship development altogether because they were unable to receive spirit communication in open circles that were dominated by the perennial issues of a handful of people. That is unfortunate.

If you have a choice of circles, I would suggest you participate in a semi-closed one. However, if you can't find a semi-closed circle, keep in mind that, depending on a circle's composition, it is probably better to participate in an open development circle than none at all.

Regardless of whether the development circle is semi-closed or open, it provides a safe environment to present evidential information and develop trust in your spirit helpers. In all cases, the mix of circle participants changes over time. This offers you the advantage of regularly working with new sitters about whom you know nothing.

Just make sure you give the development circle enough time to work! I often see student mediums drop out after they have managed to give three or four pieces of evidence on a good night. They mistakenly think that they have arrived on the hallowed stage of mediumship and they no longer need to participate in a development circle. This is the equivalent of stopping piano lessons once you've managed to play the scales or halting writing practice once you've learned to form the letters of the alphabet. Do not shortchange yourself or your spiritual gifts.

The Home Circle

Since the onset of Modern Spiritualism in 1849, home circles have been considered the key to developing mediumship. In the heyday of Spiritualism, families and friends got together a couple of times per week in one another's homes to see whether spiritual phenomena would take place. Many fine mediums developed in home circles as Spiritualism spread like wildfire across the United States. All Spiritualist mediums still honor this tradition, regardless of how many years they have been practicing.

Therefore, in addition to joining a development circle run by a professional teaching medium, I believe that students greatly benefit from participating in a home circle of like-minded individuals. This facilitates the continued opening and fine-tuning of the spiritual senses. Over time, it is the ideal setting for developing other phases of mediumship, including trance, where spirit guides speak through their mediums; transfiguration, where the spirit people overshadow the face and form of the medium so participants can recognize them; and physical phenomena, which all of the participants can perceive through the physical senses. These advanced phases of mediumship develop over the course of years, and especially in circles where participants share a mutual respect and sincerity of purpose.

Setting Up a Home Circle
Preliminary Considerations
Should the Circle Be Open or Closed?
Home circles are usually closed circles. Once the circle has formed, no new people are added unless the group gradually experiences attrition. This also means the circle's participants must choose their companions wisely. I suggest you impose a three- or four-month trial period on everyone who initially joins a home circle. That gives you the ability to turn away those who are either not committed or whose energy or disposition is not agreeable with the group.

The ideal number of participants is four to eight. It's great if there is a balance of males and females, but it is not necessary. What matters most is that the participants are dedicated, patient, and compatible. If you can only find one or two like-minded people who want to sit with you, then start your circle anyway.

How Often Should the Circle Meet?

Circles may meet weekly, every two weeks, or monthly. When you decide how frequently to meet, you should consider circle members' commute to the meeting place, especially if you live in a metropolitan area. Years ago, I participated in a circle that involved a substantial commute on the Capital Beltway. During rush hour, a one-way commute could easily turn into a two- to three-hour nightmare. To avoid arriving at the circle angry and worn out from traffic, I usually left my home before the onset of rush hour.

Be aware that most people's schedules are not amenable to such a huge commitment of time. If the commute is too far, enthusiasm wanes and people drop out. In my experience, meeting every other week is optimal. It is frequent enough so that everyone hungers for that special day, but not so often that it feels like a burden.

Home circles should always meet on the same weekday, at the same time, and at the same address, since spirit energies accumulate over time. For the same reason, it is important to insist on punctuality. Your spirit guides will prepare the space in advance and will be ready to start at the appointed time.

How Long Should the Circle Run?

Allow about ninety minutes to two hours from the opening prayer to the closing prayer, depending on the number of participants and spirit presences. This time frame allows an opportunity for feedback and sharing. You can close when all messages have been shared and when you notice the shift in energy that signals Spirit's departure. With time, you will identify a natural rhythm to your circle.

Lighting Conditions

It is not necessary to meditate in complete darkness. The famous British physical medium D. D. Home conducted his séances in full light and produced amazing phenomena. Darkness, though, can make it easier for people to relax and tune out other distractions. They might also feel less exposed in what can be a personal experience.

You might try turning out the lights and meditating by candlelight. Floating candles in a bowl with flowers can make a captivating and festive centerpiece, and can also help set a reverent, meditative mood. Salt lamps, too, cast a lovely, gentle, orange glow and make it possible to observe physical phenomena such as transfiguration and spirit lights. The spirit communicators in our Thursday night home circle have told us they utilize the ions released by the salt for the production of physical phenomena.

Eating and Drinking Before the Circle Meets

The circle participants should eat a very light meal before meetings. You should have just enough food in your stomach so you can be comfortable, but not enough to feel full. A full stomach makes it hard to shift one's awareness to the spiritual realm. You can sit with the best mediums in the world, but if all of them have full stomachs, no spirit phenomena will take place.

Circle participants should abstain from alcohol and recreational drugs before attending. These substances lower the energies of the participants. Also, high-level spirit helpers will not be attracted to mediums who get plastered before a circle. In other words, alcohol and drug use would have a negative effect on all the participants in both the physical and spirit planes.

Conducting Circle Meetings

The basic circle format is very simple: You meet, pray, meditate in silence, share spirits' messages and individual experiences, close the circle, and perhaps give one another feedback before disbanding. I have broken down the individual steps into a checklist format:

Prepare the Physical Space:

+ Before people arrive, pick up and clean the room.

+ Let in fresh air.

+ Place fresh flowers and living plants in the room.

+ Burn some sage or incense to clear the energy and set the mood.

As People Arrive:

+ Encourage them to sit quietly to help them transition from the events of the day to the sacred space of the circle.

+ Keep the conversation uplifting and pleasant. It's fine to talk about spiritual matters, but avoid discussing personal problems or the day's horror stories in the news.

+ An uplifting, devotional attitude should prevail. Sitters should be in a happy, patient, harmonious, and dedicated state of mind, looking forward to spirit contact.

When Everyone Has Arrived,
Check and Adjust the Seating Order:

+ Alternate the seating order with male and female sitters as much as possible.

+ Separate couples for optimal energy flow. Energy tends to pool and flow back and forth between people who are closely connected. This could compromise the success of a given session.

Review the Format of the Evening:

+ Explain everything from the opening prayer to the closing prayer and what happens in between.

+ Explain the length of the silent-meditation period.

+ Explain when it is appropriate for participants to give spirit messages. I recommend a quiet meditation of at least twenty to thirty minutes before any spirit messages are shared. This gives everyone enough time to unwind and become open to spirit visitors.

+ Explain whether the circle members should bring spirit greetings in a particular order or whenever they feel moved.

+ Explain there *should be absolutely no touching among the sitters after the opening prayer.* For many people, the opening prayer serves as the trigger that shifts their awareness to the spirit realms (chapter 6, "Connecting with Spirit: Shifting Your Awareness"). Experienced mediums might even be in a light trance, so when you touch a medium after the opening prayer, you are going to pull him or her out of that spirit awareness. This is very jarring to the nerves of the medium, and it may likely wreck that person's entire evening.

Opening the Circle:
Always open with an invocation, such as:

> "Infinite Spirit, thank you for joining us. Surround us with your love and light as we are gathered here tonight in our sacred circle. Open our hearts, minds, and spirits to your loving presence. Uplift us. Ennoble our spirits. We

invite our spirit guides, teachers, and loved ones, as well as all who wish to grow with us. We ask that all our spirit visitors have our highest good at heart. Thank you for expanding our spiritual perception, Great Mystery. May we continue to grow in ever-loving service to you. Amen."

Meditation:

+ Attune with the Infinite (see chapter 4, "Meditation and Attunement with the Divine").

+ Silent meditation of at least twenty to thirty minutes.

Spirit Communication and Message Sharing:
In my circles, I announce when the time has come to share messages. I let people share in whatever order they want. However, I have also been in circles where people went around the circle and when their turns came, they made their connection with the spirit world and shared what they received.

Recipients of messages should briefly acknowledge and welcome the spirit visitors conveying their message, but withhold feedback until the end of the evening.

Closing the Circle:
Always close with prayer, giving thanks for what has been given.

"Infinite Spirit, we are grateful for our time with you and with our spirit visitors. We thank you for all that has been given. Please watch over everyone as we disband and go to our homes. Until we meet again, keep us ever attuned to your loving presence and bring us opportunities to be of service to you. Thank you, Great Spirit! Amen."

Keep the lights low, and give people the chance to gradually adjust to their everyday state of consciousness.

Feedback:
Feel free to give one another feedback in the form of, "I understand the message." Or, "You were right on target." Or, "I'll have to think about that one." Or even, "I have no idea what that message or communicator is all about."

Avoid sharing your entire family and life history and providing information about spirit relatives. This undermines the purpose of the circle, as during future circles people will wonder if they are receiving information from your spirit loved ones or if they are merely working from memory.

Other Considerations
Refreshments
Food grounds energy and helps mediums reconnect with the physical realm, so you might want to offer some refreshments or share a potluck meal after meditation. This is especially important in circles where the participants are developing signs of trance or physical mediumship, or if members have a long drive ahead of them. Our Thursday night circle always concludes with a lovely potluck feast and a discussion of the evening's events and spirit messages. Initially, though, I would suggest you keep it simple and limit your offerings to water, tea, juice, fresh fruit, or cookies.

Adding New People to an Established Circle

Over time, you may find that some people drop out of your closed circle and others wish to join. Before you add newcomers to an established circle, discuss this with all circle participants. At the next circle meeting, take the question into meditation and ask Spirit's guidance. Adding another person changes the energy of the circle, for better or worse. If you decide to add another person, you might want to tell the newcomer that he or she is admitted on a trial basis until it is clear that it is a good match for the circle.

Questions & Answers

Do the spirit people follow a medium
home when the circle meeting ends?

No, they don't. The spirit people have their own lives in the spirit world, and they aren't interested in hanging around. However, I once knew a student medium who did not want to break her connection with a spirit person after the circle was over. She had been very deeply touched by the spirit visitor's life experience and continued her conversation with him during her drive home. It was her choice to continue the conversation. Had she stopped paying attention to the spirit person or had she told him to come back next week, the spirit visitor would have gone away.

Do spirit people hang around the medium after a session is over?

No, they don't. They leave with the closing prayer. If you tell the spirit people that they need to go through your gatekeeper, you will never have anyone hang around after a session is finished.

Do the spirit people come back with more
messages for the sitter after a session is finished?
No. The spirit people know when the session is over and their loved one is gone. There is no reason why they would continue to talk with the medium. Remember, mediums must practice the Law of Control and are in charge of when they open to the spirit world.

During meditation I receive a lot of information
from the spirit communicators, but when the
time comes to share, I can't remember most of it.
This happens to a lot of people. Don't worry about it. The good news is that you are connecting with Spirit. Next time, ask your spirit communicators to come back when it is time to share your message. Ask them to remind you of important parts that you need to mention. As you progress in your development, you may find you no longer need to receive information during the meditation and that Spirit shows up when it is time for you to give messages.

I've been participating in a circle for two months
now, but I'm not experiencing spirit contact.
Do you think that I'm not cut out to be a medium?
Often when people sit in home circles or in development circles and nothing seems to be happening, there is a lot going on behind the scenes that the sitter is unaware of. As far as I'm concerned, there is no such thing as an empty or wasted session, because our spirit helpers are always busy strengthening and unifying the links

between the medium and the spirit world. Remember, mediumship unfolds over time. Some people's gifts develop sooner; other people need more time. Be patient, and be gentle with yourself. Continue sitting with a pleasant and joyful attitude. Please know that your gifts will develop in their own good time. Trust in the wisdom of your spirit helpers and continue to attend the circle. I have never seen a dedicated medium whose abilities did not blossom.

Sitters in the circle don't recognize the spirit people I connect with. Congratulations, you are connecting with the spirit people! There could be several reasons why your sitters won't be able to recognize the spirit people who come to you.

First, you might not have offered enough unique evidence that would help the sitters recognize a given spirit person.

Second, you might be wrong about some of the evidence. In that case, you might want to ask if someone understands most of what you had described. If someone says, "Yes," then ask what they do understand. Then go back to your spirit link and ask for more pertinent information. Explain that you need assistance in confirming the spirit person's identity.

Third, it is entirely possible that the spirit person has no connection to anyone in the circle. The spirit people sometimes drop by out of curiosity or because they want to practice communicating with a medium. Please note: this last occurrence does not usually happen in a traditional reading where a particular sitter is asking for help. In those cases, spirit people related to the sitter are generally attracted to the experience.

Everyone in this circle is better at this than I am.

Stop comparing yourself with others. As in all areas of life, there will always be someone who manages to meditate longer, go deeper, or receive more profound insights. The problem with comparison is that it judges, measures, and finds fault with what *is*. This turns meditation and mediumship into a competitive sport instead of a spiritual experience. So don't even go there. Honor your experience and give thanks for whatever it is.

14

Nurturing Your Mediumship Over the Long Haul

Mediumship is taxing. It requires a lot of energy from the medium, especially if you are committed to practicing evidential mediumship. If you want your gift to keep growing, it is important to honor your spirit and take good care of yourself as you serve others. It is a good spiritual practice to regularly release the energy you have taken on from others.

As a medium you are naturally sensitive to other people's energy, emotions, attitudes, thoughts, hopes, and feelings. I do not believe that mediums take on the condition of the deceased's former physical experience, because the spirit body is perfect. However, as a medium you are a spiritual healer; thus you are vulnerable to the physical and emotional drain that comes with serving the bereaved and those experiencing major life turmoil.

Sensitive people often carp about their susceptibility to negative energy, but they don't realize that even when they feel great about the way they were able to help someone, they can still get bogged down with the other person's energy, even if that energy was upbeat. That is because other people's energy, whether positive or negative, is simply not available for your use, and when it accumulates in another person's energy field, it clogs spiritual channels.

Below are two processes that will help you release the energy you might have taken on from others. A third process will aid you to recover personal energy that you have scattered in the universe.

You can use these processes as often as you like. For example, you can monitor how you feel throughout each day. If you are going through a stretch where you are feeling stressed or drained, use these. Because I interact with a lot of clients during the course of my day, I tend to conduct these processes at the end of my work-week, any time I feel sluggish, or when I feel that my accuracy is off.

Take a Spiritual Cleansing Bath

A spiritual cleansing bath is a powerful way to remove the psychic sludge that has accumulated in our energy fields. Please note that this bath is not for cleaning the physical body. If your body is dirty, take a regular shower before you proceed with the spiritual cleansing bath. Also, don't add soaps, bubbles, fragrance, or oil to this bath.

Start out with a sparkling clean bathroom and bathtub. Light a couple of white candles to lift your spirits. As you fill the bathtub with warm water, adjust the temperature for your comfort and add:

+ 1 teaspoon of sea salt

+ 1 cup of apple cider vinegar

+ 2 cups of boiled white sage tea

To make the sage tea, boil several sprigs of white sage, including the stem, in 3 cups of water. When the water has reduced to about 2 cups, the tea will be ready to put in the bath.

+ Once you are in the tub, relax and focus on the purpose of the bath.

+ In prayer, ask Infinite Intelligence to cleanse away all psychic, emotional, mental, and spiritual debris that has accumulated in your energy field.

+ Pray that anything clogging your spiritual senses be washed away.

+ Fully immerse your head in the water, including your hair and face. If you cannot immerse your head, use a pitcher to pour the bath water over you.

+ With each immersion, notice how you begin to feel brighter, lighter, and clearer.

+ Stop when you feel your purpose has been accomplished.

- Drain the water.
- Rinse out your hair with clear water so the bath ingredients won't dry it out.
- Clean the bathtub once more to disperse the psychic debris you've released.
- Follow up with the Recall Your Energy Exercise.

Here is another process you can use when it is not possible to take a spiritual cleansing bath or if you just don't care for them.

Releasing Other People's Energy

- Prepare your meditation space, or, if the weather permits, perform the ceremony in a secluded place outside.
- Burn some sage and make sure you waft handfuls of the smoke over yourself, intending to release to the Great Mystery all energy that isn't yours.
- After you have burned your sage, in prayer ask the Great Mystery to cleanse away any energies and emotional burdens you have taken on from others.
- Invite your spirit helpers to assist you.
- Begin to take deep, slow, relaxed breaths. As you inhale, visualize breathing in divine life-force energy. As you exhale, push out all energies, including thoughts, emotions, and expectations that you have taken on from others.

+ Release these energies to the Great Mystery, not to
  the individuals to whom they belong.

+ Follow up with the Recall Your Energy Exercise
  (described below).

Recall Your Energy

As we go about our daily lives, we tend to give away our energy.
Every time you worry or fret about something, you give away
your energy. When you work hard on a project, you also invest
part of your life-force energy. The same is true when you have
an argument with your partner or when you are helping others.
As a medium you cannot help giving away some of your energy
to your clients. Over a period of time, you become depleted and
exhausted. It is good to periodically call back the energy you have
scattered in the universe.

+ After you have released the energies you took on from
  others, visualize a Divine Filter surrounding your
  energy field, including your head and feet.

+ Take a deep breath and begin to call back bits of
  your energy from all the people, places, projects,
  and situations where you have left it.

+ Imagine your energy is now flying through the
  universe, returning to you.

+ As you inhale, envision your energy passing through
  the Divine Filter that surrounds you. The Divine
  Filter catches and sifts out anything that isn't pure. It

heals and revitalizes your returning energy before it reenters your energy field and physical body.

+ With each exhalation, envision your returning energies being redistributed throughout your body.

+ Notice how you are beginning to feel revitalized, energized, strong, and joyful.

Maintaining Your Energy

Don't Schedule Too Many Readings

How many sitters a medium can handle varies between individuals, and it changes over time in the same individual. Mediumship is very much like a muscle that gets stronger with use. When you first go public with your gifts, you might find that your limit is one reading per week. An experienced medium might handle fifteen readings per week without compromising quality. What matters is that you honor your limits and that you don't overextend yourself. When you have worked comfortably at a given level for some months, you can increase the number of readings you give.

Have Healthy Boundaries with Sitters

It can be hard to say "No" when a distraught person calls you after hours and begs you for a reading *now*. I strongly suggest that you honor your need for downtime so you won't burn out. Just because you are a medium does not mean that you need to be on call 24/7.

Healthy boundaries also involve sticking to the scheduled length of a reading. Occasionally you are going to have a sitter who books a thirty-minute reading with you, but has enough questions to take up at least two hours of your time. Because energetically there are only so many readings that one can handle in a week and still maintain high quality, it's important to keep track of time and remain within the scheduled limits. To help you adhere to your schedule, get in the habit of asking your clients five minutes before the reading's end if they have a final question for the spirit people. This signals that time is just about up and prevents you from falling into the trap of "Just one more question."

Set a Limit on How Often You See the Same Sitter

Some people might fall in love with your work, and they may want to see you all the time if you let them. The problem is that this creates an unhealthy dependency in the sitter as well as a huge emotional and energetic drain on you. No matter how much we miss our departed loved ones, we have to learn to live without their physical presence. Mastering loss and bereavement is part of life, and your ability to connect with specific departed spirit people loses its beneficial effects for the living people who are so desperate for connection. I do not read for my clients more than twice per year. If necessary, however, I explain that too-frequent sessions diminish the experience.

Release the Readings You Have Given

It is only natural that we want to remember the highlights of the evidential reading we have given. However, it is best to let each reading flow through you just as water flows through a straw. When the reading is done and your sitter leaves, release the memories of the sitting and the astounding evidence the spirit people have brought. In this way, the next time the person comes to see you, you will be able to work with a fresh spirit link instead of having memories from the previous reading get in your way.

I begin the letting-go process the moment I make the closing prayer. When I blow out the candle I lit at the beginning of the sitting, I release all memories of the reading. Within thirty minutes of blowing out the candle, I only remember a small fraction of what came through, and after an hour I don't remember anything. Sometimes this is confusing to my sitters, who might see me again and refer to something that was said the last time we met. Or if I read for friends, they assume that I know things about them that I actually do not. Be sure to explain these circumstances, because this ensures that the sitter's experiences are private, even if you are there in the moment of transmission.

Spend Time in Nature

There is nothing like the healing power of nature to restore body, mind, and spirit, and facilitate the awakening of the spiritual senses. If possible, go on a hike, or simply work or sit in your garden. It's good to be in the woods, regardless of the season. Nature has many lessons to impart. Let the wind blow away your worries, and let the sunshine lift your spirits. Lie down on Mother Earth, and let her recharge you.

Avoid Becoming a Spiritual Junkie

No one can live around the clock in the higher vibrations of the spirit world. When a medium's spiritual gifts begin to unfold, they often take workshop after workshop without allowing time in between to absorb the material that was presented. It's easy to become a spiritual junkie, searching for one spiritual high after another. This kind of pursuit cannot sustain itself and detracts from the experience you are trying to have.

Enjoy Your Life

We are on earth to enjoy life in the physical realm. So do give yourself periodic downtime, a break from all things spiritual. I am not saying to abandon your spiritual practice. You should never abandon prayer and meditation! But be sure to make time for outings with friends, enjoying family, going to the movies, reading a novel, sleeping in late, and going to the beach. Just be a person, not a medium.

15

The Natural Cycles of Mediumship Development

Just as the year has the seasons of spring, summer, fall, and winter, the unfolding of mediumship, too, moves in predictable cycles. There are four parts to each cycle: expansion, consolidation, rest, and contraction. These cycles will repeat many times through our work as mediums, as we are initiated into deeper understandings and greater sensitivity. This is true for all mediums, no matter how long they have been practicing.

Expansion

During periods of expansion you will typically experience rapid growth. It seems like each meditation brings awesome insights. In circles, public demonstrations, or work with clients, you are able to bring through phenomenal evidence. You might feel like you are making significant progress toward your goals as a medium. During this time, you might also feel as if you are able to see spirit through a microscope: everything looks large and magnified. This period of expansion can last several weeks to several months before you enter a period of consolidation.

Consolidation

When you reach a consolidation period, you are probably happy with your mediumship, and you maintain the accomplishment of the period of expansion. You probably feel quite confident in the growth you have experienced. During consolidation, meditations tend to be peaceful and refreshing. We might experience less conscious spirit contact, but that is fine with us since we continue to be aware of the close contact with our spirit guides. During consolidation, you will still receive fresh insights and perspectives, though not as often or as profoundly as you did during the period of expansion.

Rest

Expansion and consolidation are followed by a period of rest. These times invariably feel as if you have hit a plateau. Try as you might, your mediumship does not seem to grow anymore, and you probably experience a sense of stagnation. During rest periods, we can grow terribly bored with meditation and with development or the home circles we attend. Day after day of receiving nothing can make us wonder if we really have any talent at all and whether our earlier growth was just blind luck.

In these moments, keep in mind that times of rest occur because there are usually other factors in your life that need to come into balance. Your new spiritual understanding has probably inspired significant changes in your life. There might be new relationships, jobs, or new places of residence to adjust to. Rest periods can last many months to several years.

Over the years, I have learned to recognize rest periods in my mediumship development as a reminder that I do live on earth and that there are things that I need to take care of. I find that rest periods are easier to handle when I engage in regular physical exercise.

This is also a good time to review the natural laws that govern mediumship and to redouble our efforts to apply them. I often manage to get myself out of a slump by volunteering more of my time to worthwhile causes. Amazingly, as I focus on serving others, my mediumship begins to bloom again—and I realize the slump is not as bad as I thought.

Contraction

You can tell you have reached the end of a rest when you hit the period of contraction. Invariably, during contraction, it appears as if your mediumship is sliding backward. You might be unable to achieve the same level of evidence or accuracy that you previously reached. You might even feel blocked in your ability to communicate with spirit.

Periods of contraction are usually painful, and they often coincide with a letting-go process in other areas of our life. While intensely uncomfortable and frustrating, periods of contraction don't last very long, usually no more than several weeks at most.

The important thing to remember is that during periods of contraction, our spirit guides are usually working extra hard in preparing us for the next period of expansion. Rest up, and accept and honor this stage of mediumship. Do not become too pushy or too demanding of yourself or of your spirit guides.

I like to think of the period of contraction as the time when my guides have taken my mediumship "network" down to install an "upgrade." Remember, when you download new updates for your computer, your computer is temporarily unable to perform its usual functions. The same is true for mediumship. Once the new network has been installed, you will be bursting into your next period of expansion and you will be able to operate with increased "bandwidth."

Continue with your prayers, daily meditation, and regular physical exercise. Trust that all is as it needs to be. Resist the temptation to be hard on yourself. But most of all, don't give up.

Conclusion

I hope this book will remain your companion throughout your journey to become a full-fledged medium. Continue to put the practices and exercises to good use. And always remember, just as when you learn to play the guitar, you are going to hit bum notes in your developing mediumship. Do not let those moments discourage you. Be willing to take risks and make mistakes, and know that you will perfect your skills with practice.

Find a development circle or start a home circle. Take classes or workshops with qualified teachers. If you are stuck in the middle of nowhere, start an online group, such as through Meetup or Yahoo. It's definitely possible to successfully meditate with others over the telephone or Skype once a week. I offer long-distance development circles via conference call for those who are unable to attend my circles in the Washington, DC area.

Please realize that over time as you unfold your abilities, more spirit people will be drawn to your inner spiritual light. On extremely rare occasions you could encounter a spirit person who is stuck on the lower astral realms and needs help reuniting with his or her spirit loved ones.

This has happened to me a couple of times and it is nothing to worry about. It is similar to encountering a person in the physical realm who got lost and is asking for directions. It is important to realize that a stuck spirit person is generally not evil. There are many reasons why a spirit person can unwittingly get stuck. You will find the tools that you need to help such a person in appendix A, "Earthbound Spirits and Conducting Spirit Rescue."

Please know there are experienced mediums who can assist you, if needed. The silver lining to these moments is that you can help people on both sides of the veil.

The path of the medium is a lifelong journey. It allows you to be a light in the life of others and to help them through some of life's rough patches. It gives you glimpses of eternity that will often make your daily concerns seem very small and very manageable. Ultimately, first-hand knowledge of the continuity of life beyond physical death will help you lead a good, purposeful, and meaningful life.

I wish you all the best with many blessings on your journey.

Appendix A
Earthbound Spirits and Conducting Spirit Rescue

Earthbound spirit people are stuck on the astral plane closest to Earth due to their own level of consciousness. When people die, their consciousness is still the same as it was when they were incarnated on Earth. There are many reasons why spirit people can get lost or stuck and unable to move to the other side. Understanding these reasons can assist you in dealing with interactions with spirit people in this condition.

They Might Not Realize They Are No Longer in Their Physical Bodies

The transition from this life to the next can be so smooth and seamless that the dying person might not realize they have passed on. I had a friend who fell into this category. A lifelong devout Christian, he expected Jesus to meet him at the gates of heaven. Because he had not met Jesus, he didn't think he had crossed over. He became frustrated when he found himself unable to communicate with his wife and children. When he finally came to see me, he was furious—because to him, it seemed that his loved ones were purposefully ignoring him. It took me a good thirty minutes to convince him that he had indeed died and gone to Spirit. Months later, he visited me again to thank me for my help.

Death Was Sudden or Violent

People who died suddenly or violently can be unaware of the fact they've made their transition, like Bruce Willis's character in the movie *The Sixth Sense*. This can apply to suicides, those who died in natural disasters, soldiers who died in war, murder victims, and those who had a heart attack or died in a car accident. These circumstances are polar opposites of the smooth transition that is seamless for the deceased, but the result can be the same. However, just because someone died suddenly or violently does not necessarily mean they are going to be lost or stuck.

Unfinished Business or Concern for Loved Ones Left Behind

Sometimes people die without having the opportunity to finish up all of their business here on earth. There might be dependent loved ones left behind, especially young children with no reliable caretaker to depend upon. In such cases, the departed person can be so worried and concerned about their loved ones that they will stay close, losing sight of the fact that eventually they need to move on with their life in the spirit world.

They Experience Attachment to Familiar Surroundings

Sometimes spirit people loved their homes and physical surroundings so much that they seek to stay in the places that were so dear to them. Sometimes they still have a feeling of ownership for the place they used to live and make their presence known to others who have moved into the space.

They Believe in Hell and Fear Punishment in Death

Those who didn't live a clean life and have a strong belief in a place called hell might prefer to cling to the astral plane closest to earth for fear of eternal condemnation.

Because of a Belief System, They Cannot Perceive Spirit Helpers

As I illustrated in the example of my angry, rejected friend, some people have very rigid ideas of what is supposed to happen after death. If they do not encounter what they expect, they won't accept that they have crossed over. It could be the idea that they are going to be met by Jesus, and when Jesus fails to appear they don't think they've passed on. They don't know what has happened, but they certainly don't think they are deceased. Others believe they are supposed to sleep until Jesus awakens them on Judgment Day. It behooves all of us to keep an open mind about what we might find on the other side after we leave our bodies.

They Experienced Addictions in Life

Attachment to drugs, alcohol, smoking, food, sex, gambling, and other earthly desires can exert a powerful hold on a spirit entity's ability to move forward on the other side. Some addicts indeed choose to stay close to the earthly realms so they can vicariously continue to enjoy their favorite fixes.

It is important to remember that these earthbound spirit entities are not evil. As we have seen, for the most part they are stuck because they simply don't know any better.

Some Are Simply Mischievous

There are mischievous spirit people just as there are pranksters and mischievous people here on earth. And remember, physical death does not bestow instant spiritual elevation. A mischievous spirit person can act inappropriately and require your intervention. They might touch us inappropriately or create sounds, smells, or images that are distasteful and off-putting. For the most part, though, these are cries for help from a soul that has tried everything and has simply run out of ideas. Very few spirit people actually intend to scare the medium.

The key to dealing with a mischievous spirit person is to avoid being scared or taken in by their attempts to impress you. Let the entity know you are aware of what they are up to and tell them to go to the light. Be firm in your tone and demeanor. There is no reason for you to put up with inappropriate behavior from anyone, living or dead.

You can also ask if they want you to help them move on. If someone you know is being harassed by a mischievous spirit person, you can conduct a spirit rescue circle meeting. Sometimes spirit people need the help of mediums on earth before they can be reunited with their spirit loved ones, even though there are emergency spirit helpers and guides on the other side who look for stuck spirit people in need of assistance.

Sometimes, though, a spirit person's state of consciousness prevents him or her from being able to perceive the spirit helpers nearby. In such cases, mediums on the earth plane are often better able to assist the earthbound spirit.

How to Conduct a Spirit Rescue

Spirit rescue is an advanced topic in mediumship, and I do not recommend that absolute beginners try their hands at this. However, if you have been sitting in a development circle for some time and have become proficient in your ability to connect with the spirit world, then you might be put in a situation where you'll have to conduct a spirit rescue.

To handle this situation, get together with like-minded people from your development circle or home circle. Remember, when people meditate together in a circle, the combined energies of the sitters and guides facilitate a powerful and positive experience.

Before conducting the spirit rescue, thoroughly smudge the meeting place with sage. Open the windows, and sweep the smoke from the burning sage toward the open windows. After you have smudged and aired out the house, close the windows. Set up chairs in a circle, following the directions for setting up a home circle in chapter 13, "Development Circles and Home Circles".

When everyone has arrived, begin the session with prayer, stating the reason for the gathering. Ask for assistance for the suffering spirit person, so he or she can move ahead on a path of evolution and be reunited with deceased loved ones and guides. Invite your spirit guides and spirit helpers to join you in assisting the spirit entity to find its way to the light. After the prayer, enter your meditative state and stay open to what happens.

If the spirit person approaches you, ask why he or she is here and how you might help. Ask if he or she is afraid of anything. More than likely, the spirit person will go right ahead and share a sad story with you. During the course of the conversation, you can direct the person toward spirit guides and spirit loved ones.

Ask the earthbound spirit person to look around and notice spirit helpers and loved ones waiting to assist. Once these loved ones are noticed, the stuck person usually takes off, and that's it.

Some, however, might be hesitant to join their spirit helpers out of fear. In that case, you'll have to talk with the earthbound spirit person and soothe any specific concerns. Point out the love that you can perceive as coming from spirit guides and spirit loved ones waiting in the wings. Explain that there is no hell and no eternal damnation. Explain that spirit guides and loved ones will take good care of the stuck spirit and that it is safe to go with them.

You might have to spend some time with spirit people in this dilemma, but ultimately they will be able to process what you are saying and will become ready to move on. Just be friendly, kind, and patient with them.

After a spirit person has departed with his or her loved ones, close the circle with a prayer of gratitude for the assistance that has been given, and ask that the departed spirit person continue to progress in the spirit world. Turn on the lights, open the windows, and smudge again with sage.

Appendix B
Practices, Exercises, Meditations, and Processes

Practices for the Natural Laws

Monitor Your Vibration through Self-Observation

Review Your Connections

Release Fear-Based Thoughts, Attitudes, Memories, and Experiences

Make Positive Affirmations

Observe Yourself

Discover Motivation

Incorporate Service into Your Daily Life

Locate Unconditional Love

Track Efforts and Results

Find the On/Off Switch

Conduct Daily Meditation and Prayer

Prayer Practices

Practice Gratitude

Ask the Great Spirit to Awaken Your Heart in Love

Go into Nature for Sunset Prayers

Make Evening Prayers in the Deep Woods

Take a Sacred Walk

Pray for Everyone

Pray Everywhere

Write Your Prayers

Decree Blessings

Meditation for Spirit Communication

Step 1: Relaxing the Body

Step 2: Centering

Step 3: Focusing on the Breath

Step 4: Blend Earth and Divine Energy

Step 5: Attunement with the Divine

Exercise: Counting Backward

Exercise: Chanting "Ohm"

Exercise: Incorporate a Mantra to Stay Focused

The Spiritual Senses

To Foster Clairvoyance

People-Watching through the Compassionate Heart

Picture the Face of a Loved One in Your Mind's Eye

Sending and Receiving Visual Images

To Foster Clairaudience

Listen to the Sounds of Nature

Listen Carefully to Music and Try to Identify the
    Individual Instruments

Broaden Your Musical Listening Range

Exchange Telepathic Verbal Messages with a Friend

To Foster Clairsentience

Practice Clairsentience with Trees

People-Watching with Clairsentience

Exchange Feelings with a Friend

Expanding Your Sensitivity and Emotional Vocabulary

Clairsentience in Traffic

Activity with a Group and a Blindfold

To Foster Claircognizance
Claircognizance in Your Daily Life

To Foster Clairolfaction
Notice the Smells and Scents in the Physical Realm

Ask Your Spirit Helpers to Bring You a Fragrance

To Foster Clairgustation
Pay Attention to Taste Sensations in the Physical Realm

Tasting Foods While Blindfolded

Step 6: Notice What You See, Hear, Sense, Feel, Smell, and Taste

Exercises to Shift Your Awareness and Connect with the Spirit World
Practice: Becoming Aware of Your Own Spirit

Step 7: Extend Your Awareness Beyond Your Body

Step 8: Send Love to the Spirit People

Exercise: Playing Pretend

Connecting with Your Spirit Guides
Process 1: Meet a Spirit Guide

Process 2: Thinning the Veils of Separation

Practices to Deepen Your Connection with Your Guides

Get in the Habit of Asking for Help

Ask Your Guides for a Gift

Ask Your Guides for a Message from Your Environment

Ask Your Guides for a Message from a Book

Is It Spirit Communication or Imagination?

Exercise: How to Distinguish True and False Information

Ping-Pong with Spirit: The Process of Receiving Spirit Communication

Step 9: Begin a Mental Dialogue with the Spirit People

Exercise: Give Your Spirit Guides Feedback

Symbolism Exercises

Discover the Meaning of Symbols through Journaling

Choose a Symbol to Represent Various Situations in Your Life

Symbol Assessment Reading

Take a Symbol Divination Walk

Glossary

Clairaudience: A medium's ability to hear the voices, sounds, and messages from the spirit world with the inner, spiritual ear.

Claircognizance: A medium's ability to suddenly know complex information, concepts, and ideas without prior instruction or consultation of mundane sources of information.

Clairgustation: A medium's ability to taste the foods that the spirit people enjoyed during their life on earth.

Clairolfaction: A medium's ability to smell the odors and scents connected with a spirit person.

Clairsentience: A medium's ability to sense the physical conditions and emotions projected by spirit people.

Clairvoyance: The ability to receive visual impulses such as pictures, symbols, or images that are sent by spirit communicators.

Development circle: A group of student mediums who meet under the tutelage of an experienced medium for the purpose of developing their mediumship.

Earthbound spirit: Deceased person who got stuck in the lower astral realm after death.

Gatekeeper: A spirit guide who controls the spirit people's access to a medium.

Great Mystery: The impersonal, creative force of the universe that permeates everything that exists.

Great Spirit: See Great Mystery.

Home circle: A group of mediums or student mediums who meet regularly in one person's home for the purpose of connecting with the spirit people.

Infinite Intelligence: See Great Mystery.

Lower astral realm: The transitional zone between Earth and the spirit world.

Medium: A person who is sensitive to the presence of the spirit people and through whose instrumentality the spirit people are able to communicate with the people incarnated on Earth.

Mediumship: The process through which communication between the people on Earth and the people in heaven takes place.

Mental mediumship: The process through which a medium perceives the spirit people through the spiritual senses. Only the medium, and not the sitter, is able to perceive the presence of the spirit people through mental mediumship.

Natural law: The laws that govern the universe. Both the physical world and the spirit world are governed by the same set of laws.

Physical phenomena: Sound and manifestations produced by the spirit people that all the sitters in a séance are able to perceive through their five physical senses.

Precognition: A form of claircognizance defined as foreknowledge of future events without input from mundane sources of information.

Premonition: A form of claircognizance that differs from precognition in that it contains an element of forewarning or danger.

Reading: A consultation between a sitter and a medium for the purpose of contacting the sitter's deceased loved ones.

Recipient: The person who receives spirit communication through a medium in a public mediumship demonstration or in a private reading.

Séance: A gathering of people around a medium for the purpose of contacting the spirit world.

Séance room: The room where a séance is held.

Sitter: A person who seeks out the services of a medium.

Spirit communicator: The spirit person who is in the process of conveying information to a medium.

Spirit entities: See spirit people.

Spirit guides: Spirit people who help humans on their journey through life and who help mediums connect with the spirit world.

Spirit helpers: People in the spirit world who help humans and mediums with a variety of life tasks.

Spirit people/spirit person: Deceased people who once lived on Earth and now live in the spirit world.

Spirit rescue: The process through which a medium helps a spirit person who is stuck in the lower astral realm fully transition to the spirit world.

Spirit world: The place where people, animals, and plants go after they die, also known as heaven.

Spiritual senses: The inner senses through which a medium is able to perceive the spirit world; includes clairaudience, claircognizance, clairgustation, clairolfaction, clairsentience, and clairvoyance.

Trance: A phase of mediumship in which the spirit guides and spirit people speak directly through a medium.

Transfiguration: A phase of mediumship in which the spirit people overshadow the face, features, and possibly the body of the medium with their own appearance.

Vibration: The unseen spiritual energy of all living things on earth and in the spirit world.

Bibliography

Alexander, Eben. *Proof of Heaven: A Neurosurgeon's Journey into the Afterlife.* Simon & Schuster. 2012.

Alexander, Stewart. *An Extraordinary Journey: The Memoirs of a Physical Medium.* Saturday Night Press. 2010.

Ávila, Teresa of. *The Book of My Life.* Translated by Mirabai Starr. New Seeds Books. 2007.

Barbanell, Maurice. *Power of the Spirit.* Psychic Press. 1989.

Blum, Deborah. *Ghost Hunters: William James and the Search for Scientific Proof of Life After Death.* Penguin Press. 2006.

Borgia, Anthony. *Life in the World Unseen.* M.A.P. Inc. 1993.

Burney, Diana. *Spiritual Clearings: Sacred Practices to Release Negative Energy and Harmonize Your Life.* North Atlantic Books. 2009.

Cayce, Edgar. *A Search for God Books I & II*. A.R.E. Press. 2011.

Colburn, Nettie. *Nettie Colburn Trance Medium: The Autobiography of the Medium Who Gave Trance Sittings to Abraham Lincoln*. SNU Publications. 2009.

Crookes, William. *Researches in the Phenomena of Spiritualism*. The Quarterly Journal of Science. 1874.

Davich, Victor. *8 Minute Meditation: Quiet Your Mind. Change Your Life*. Penguin Group. 2004.

Fiore, Edith. *The Unquiet Dead: A Psychologist Treats Spirit Possession*. Ballantine Books. 1987.

Kornfield, Jack. *A Path with Heart: A Guide Through the Perils and Promises of Spiritual Life*. Bantam Books. 1993.

Matthews, Caitlin. *Psychic Shield: The Personal Handbook of Psychic Protection*. Ulysses Press. 2006.

Moorjani, Anita. *Dying To Be Me: My Journey from Cancer, to Near Death, to True Healing*. Hay House, Inc. 2012.

Morris Pratt Institute. Educational Course on Modern Spiritualism. 2001.

Myers, F.W.H. *Human Personality and Its Survival of Bodily Death*. Hampton Roads Publishing Company, Inc. 2001.

National Spiritualist Association of Churches. *NSAC Spiritualist Manual*. 2004.

Radin, Dean. *The Conscious Universe: The Scientific Truth of Psychic Phenomena*. Harper Edge. 1997.

Roberts, Estelle. *Fifty Years a Medium*. SNU Publications. 2006.

Schwartz, Gary E. *The Afterlife Experiments: Breakthrough Scientific Evidence of Life After Death*. Atria Books. 2002.

Schwartz, Gary E. *The Sacred Promise: How Science Is Discovering Spirit's Collaboration with Us in Our Daily Lives*. Atria Books. 2011.

Solomon, Grant, and Jane Solomon, in association with The Scole Experimental Group. *The Scole Experiment: Scientific Evidence for Life After Death*. Piatkus Publishing. 1999.

Speck, Frank G. *Naskapi: The Savage Hunters of the Labrador Peninsula*. University of Oklahoma Press. 1977.

Stevens, José Luis. *Praying With Power: How to Use Ancient Shamanic Techniques to Gain Maximum Spiritual Benefit and Extraordinary Results Through Prayer*. Watkins Publishing. 2005.

Tomkins, Ptolemy. *The Modern Book of the Dead: A Revolutionary Perspective on Death, the Soul, and What Really Happens in the Life to Come*. Atria Books. 2012.

Tuttle, Hudson. *Mediumship and Its Laws: Its Conditions and Cultivation*. 98th edition. National Spiritualist Association of Churches.

Wallis, E. W. *A Guide to Mediumship and Psychical Unfoldment.* Kessinger Publishing.

Weisberg, Barbara. *Talking to the Dead: Kate and Maggie Fox and the Rise of Spiritualism.* Harper San Francisco. 2004.

White, Stewart Edward. *The Betty Book.* Ariel Press. 1988.

Wickland, Carl A. *Thirty Years Among the Dead.* Newcastle Publishing Company. 1974.

Yogananda, Paramahansa. *Man's Eternal Quest: Collected Talks and Essays on Realizing God in Daily Life.* Self-Realization Fellowship. 2008.

To Write the Author

If you wish to contact the author or would like more information about this book, please write to the author in care of Llewellyn Worldwide, and we will forward your request. We cannot guarantee that every letter written to the author can be answered, but all will be forwarded. Please write to:

Konstanza Morning Star
℅ Llewellyn Worldwide
2143 Wooddale Drive
Woodbury, MN 55125-2989

Please enclose a self-addressed stamped envelope for reply, or $1.00 to cover costs. If outside the USA, enclose an international postal reply coupon.

GET MORE AT LLEWELLYN.COM

Visit us online to browse hundreds of our books and decks, plus sign up to receive our e-newsletters and exclusive online offers.

- Free tarot readings • Spell-a-Day • Moon phases
- Recipes, spells, and tips • Blogs • Encyclopedia
- Author interviews, articles, and upcoming events

GET SOCIAL WITH LLEWELLYN

Find us on Facebook

www.Facebook.com/LlewellynBooks

Follow us on

www.Twitter.com/Llewellynbooks

GET BOOKS AT LLEWELLYN

LLEWELLYN ORDERING INFORMATION

Order online: Visit our website at www.llewellyn.com to select your books and place an order on our secure server.

Order by phone:
- Call toll free within the U.S. at 1-877-NEW-WRLD (1-877-639-9753)
- Call toll free within Canada at 1-866-NEW-WRLD (1-866-639-9753)
- We accept VISA, MasterCard, American Express and Discover

Order by mail:
Send the full price of your order (MN residents add 6.875% sales tax) in U.S. funds, plus postage and handling to: Llewellyn Worldwide, 2143 Wooddale Drive, Woodbury, MN 55125-2989

POSTAGE AND HANDLING:
STANDARD: (U.S. & Canada)
(Please allow 12 business days)
$30.00 and under, add $4.00.
$30.01 and over, FREE SHIPPING.

INTERNATIONAL ORDERS:
$16.00 for one book, plus $3.00 for each additional book.

Visit us online for more shipping options. Prices subject to change.

FREE CATALOG!

To order, call
1-877-NEW-WRLD
ext. 8236
or visit our
website

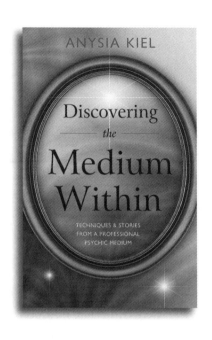

ANYSIA KIEL

Discovering
the
Medium
Within

TECHNIQUES & STORIES
FROM A PROFESSIONAL
PSYCHIC MEDIUM

Discovering the Medium Within

Techniques & Stories from
a Professional Psychic Medium
ANYSIA KIEL

Anysia Kiel invites us to witness the wondrous, dramatic, and truly beautiful moments that have shaped her life as a psychic medium. Her powerful life story—communicating with deceased family members and friends to bring comfort, healing, and peace to the living—will inspire you to embark on your own journey of psychic awakening.

Seeing spirits everywhere—in her bedroom at night, on buses and streets, and in graveyards—was terrifying for young Anysia. Then one day her own grandmother in spirit reached out to her, giving Anysia the strength and courage to begin a journey of self discovery that forever changed her life. Discover how she learns, with help from her spirit guides, how to develop and control her profound gift for spirit communication and energy healing. Her touching story, filled with miraculous spiritual encounters, concludes with Anysia's personal techniques for psychic development to help you reunite with your own loved ones in spirit.

978-0-7387-3667-9, 240 pp., 5³⁄₁₆ x 8   **$14.99**

To order, call 1-877-NEW-WRLD
Prices subject to change without notice
Order at Llewellyn.com 24 hours a day, 7 days a week

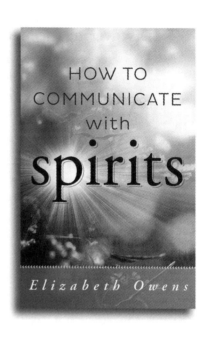

HOW TO
COMMUNICATE
with
spirits

Elizabeth Owens

How to Communicate with Spirits
Elizabeth Owens

Nowhere else will you find such a wealth of anecdotes from noted professional mediums residing within a Spiritualist community. These real-life psychics shed light on spirit entities, spirit guides, relatives who are in spirit, and communication with all of those on the spirit side of life.

You will explore the different categories of spirit guidance, and you will hear from the mediums themselves about their first contacts with the spirit world, as well as the various phenomena they have encountered.

- ◆ Noted Spiritualist mediums share their innermost experiences, opinions, and advice regarding spirit communication

- ◆ Includes instructions for table tipping, automatic writing, and meditating to contact spirits

- ◆ For anyone interested in developing and understanding spiritual gifts

978-1-56718-530-0, 216 pp., 5³⁄₁₆ x 8   **$14.99**

To order, call 1-877-NEW-WRLD
Prices subject to change without notice
Order at Llewellyn.com 24 hours a day, 7 days a week